The Pastor as Servant

PASTORAL MINISTRY SERIES

(A series for pastors and laypeople, which addresses the nature
and scope of ministry as a task of the congregation)

The Pastor as Prophet
The Pastor as Servant

The Pastor as Servant

EDITED BY

Earl E. Shelp
and
Ronald H. Sunderland

The Pilgrim Press
NEW YORK

Library of Congress Cataloging-in-Publication Data

Main entry under title:

The Pastor as servant.

 Bibliography: p.
 Contents: The servant dimension of pastoral ministry in Biblical perspective/Paul D. Hanson—The character of servanthood/Ronald H. Sunderland—Justice and the servant task of pastoral ministry/Tom F. Driver—[etc.]
 1. Pastoral theology—Addresses, essays, lectures.
2. Service (Theology)—Addresses, essays, lectures.
I. Shelp, Earl E., 1947–   II. Sunderland, Ronald, 1929–
BV4011.P335   1986   253   85-28447
ISBN 0-8298-0580-X

The Pilgrim Press, 132 West 31 Street, New York, NY 10001

Contents

Acknowledgments

The essays presented in this volume were originally presented during the spring of 1985 as the Parker Lectures in Theology and Ministry at the Institute of Religion in Houston, Texas. The Henderson-Wessendorf Foundation generously provided a grant to underwrite this second annual series of lectures. This support is gratefully acknowledged. The Institute's new director, J. Robert Nelson, and the Board of Trustees warrant recognition and appreciation for their part in the lectures and production of this book. The contributors did double duty, making outstanding oral presentations and producing manuscripts in a timely fashion. Marjory Bottoms assisted in the preparation of the final drafts of manuscripts. In addition to the individuals already named, the editors express their gratitude to Marion M. Meyer of the Pilgrim Press for her dedication to and labors in behalf of this project.

Mr. R.A. Parker, for whom the annual Parker Lectures are named, died March 21, 1985. Beginning in 1986, the annual series will be designated the Parker Memorial Lectures in Theology and Ministry. The contribution of Mr. Parker to the life of the church and to the ministry of the Institute of Religion will be perpetuated in this manner.

Introduction

Earl E. Shelp and Ronald H. Sunderland

THE ESSAYS IN THIS VOLUME EXAMINE THE SERVANT TASK
of pastoral ministry. Previous volumes by the editors focused
on a biblical basis[1] and the prophetic[2] dimension of pastoral
ministry. A subsequent volume will explore the priestly aspect of pastoral ministry.[3] The selection of the servant, prophetic, and priestly functions of pastoral ministry for
contemporary examination was not arbitrary. These functions
coincide with the "three offices" of Christ used by theologians
for centuries to explain the person and work of Jesus. If
Christian ministry is to be an extension of Jesus' ministry,
then it is important for people who minister to understand the
foundation for their activity and the generic forms that that
activity might properly take.

The offices of Christ as prophet, priest, and king have been
revised in this series on pastoral ministry to substitute the
term servant for "king." This translation is necessary, since
the primary concern here is on a task of ministry, rather than
on the person of the one who ministers. The translation also
may be valid christologically. After the death of Jesus and
belief in his resurrection became fixed among early Chris-

Earl E. Shelp, Ph.D., is Research Fellow, Institute of Religion, and
assistant professor of medical ethics, Baylor College of Medicine, Houston,
Texas.

Ronald H. Sunderland, Ed.D., is Research Fellow, Institute of Religion,
Houston, Texas.

tians, his ontological and functional unity with God was perceived. From this perspective it was considered appropriate to extend Jesus' sovereignty or kingship backward to the period of his earthly existence,[4] rather than to ascribe sovereignty to him only at the point of his exaltation. During his life, however, Jesus is presented in the New Testament as a "servant of the Lord," a role that is analogous, for example, to the relation between Israel's kings and Yahweh. The title servant described the character of Jesus' activity in relation to God. Understood in this fashion, "Jesus as servant" becomes preliminary and necessary to the designation of "Jesus as king." The terminological shift effected by the early church is profoundly important.[5] It reflects not only a developed understanding of the person of Jesus, but also a perception of human character and conduct that is eminently acceptable to God. Thus, the reversed, functional translation in this volume from "king" to "servant" represents an effort to focus on that aspect of Jesus' kingship that people who confess him as Lord (Christ, King, Messiah) are obliged to replicate. This emphasis may be unprecedented. Nevertheless, we believe that not only is it accurate, but also essential if the kingly office of Christ is to inform the ministry of contemporary believers.

W.A. Visser 't Hooft wrote *The Kingship of Christ* after World War II.[6] This small but powerfully written volume was a response to Nazism and the state of the church in Europe at that time. Visser 't Hooft reminded his readers that Jesus is Lord, rather than some demonic pretender. He cited the dangers that attend a restriction of the realm of Jesus' lordship to the church, and not to the societal structures of which the church is a part. He drew attention to the excesses and evils that can proliferate in a world governed by people without reference to God. The individualism and pietism that Visser 't Hooft identified as deflecting the attention of God's people away from their true master in that era are prospectively equally powerful today to lead Christians to misidentify their master and misunderstand the nature of servanthood. Like

Christians of an earlier generation, perhaps we need to be reminded that God is true authority, that our relation to the Holy One is properly servanthood and not privilege. Perhaps the time is again right to be reminded that the priorities of the people of God, of God's servants, ought to be set by the gospel and not by culture. If these truths are forgotten, if these emphases are neglected, the lure of false masters may grow stronger, and counterfeit forms of servanthood may result.

The people of God, the church, should learn a lesson from the history out of which Visser 't Hooft spoke. The Christian church must ever be faithful to the one whose name it bears. Its attention ought to be fixed on its Master, and its activity ought to conform to the divine mission, despite the temptations to do otherwise or the dangers that are associated with faithfulness. In order for the church's witness to be genuine, it must be clear about its own identity. The corporate church and the individuals who constitute it must acknowledge that they belong to God and that they are God's servants. When the people of God are clear about this, the role and function in the world to which they are called become clear—they are to serve God, revealed in the person and work of Jesus. In their corporate and individual confession that Jesus is Lord, a powerful polemic against any and all false contenders for loyalty is issued. By maintaining a single-minded service to God, the opportunity to serve a false master decreases accordingly.

A simple yet vital message filters through Visser 't Hooft's analysis of Christ's kingship and, derivatively, the meaning of servanthood: being a servant of the Lord entails a concern for the well-being of individual persons and the social order. In short, servanthood is person-centered and, at the same time, intensely aware of the impact of social injustice on personal need. Servant ministry includes and is more than "visiting the sick" (Matthew 25), for example. It seeks justice and righteousness as social norms (cf. Isaiah 16:5). Each form of servant ministry complements and contributes to the other.

xi

Regardless of which form servant ministry takes, each is service to God, on whose behalf the servant acts.

Like the kings of Israel, who were seen to have a position of responsibility under God, the servants of God are charged to be faithful instruments of God. The servant church must have a living relation to God. A "church" that does not assume the role of God's servant ceases to be the people of God. As Visser 't Hooft observed, without this identity the "church" is no longer the *ecclesia;* it becomes only a "human association for the maintenance of spiritual ideas and moral standards."[7] Servant ministry, like the gospel by which its priorities are set, is inclusive. The church, when functioning rightly, ought to be mobilized for God's service, reaching out to people and powers from which it has been separated. By so doing the servant church is a sign of the unity and universality of the realm of God. By prophetic proclamation of the word and by priestly prayer, service to God is rendered. By witness and example, the truth, as it is perceived by the people of God, is conveyed to those who serve other masters. The central question here is not who is Master. The answer is unequivocal in Christian theology—Jesus is Lord. There are two questions, however, that may be more vexing for people who make this confession: Will we live as servants of the Lord, and how should we live as servants of the Lord? The essays in this book address these two equally critical features of servanthood.

Paul Hanson sets the role and tasks of servanthood in biblical perspective. He examines the religious and political backgrounds from which the Hebraic use of the term slave (servant) was drawn. The people of Yahweh were reminded constantly that the question was not whether an individual or nation would serve a master, but which master each would choose to serve. The primitive church was confronted with a similar choice. They could serve either sin or righteousness. The former course is said to lead to death and destruction. The latter course is said to lead to freedom and life. By faith in God through Christ one rejects service to sin and becomes a slave to righteousness. Hanson notes that in the washing of the feet, the disciples were taught by example the secret that in bondage to God, true freedom is found. Service to God, in New Testament perspective, is expressed by means of loving service to others out of a primary devotion to God. Seen in this light, servanthood is a "life prepared to empathize and to suffer by a love that unites all those loved by God in a sense of faithful solidarity." Hanson suggests that the contemporary church faces the same choice and opportunity that the primitive church faced. Its mission, like that of the first Christians, is to present an alternate loyalty to people who are bound to false gods. By so doing, Christians become agents of healing and deliverance. Their witness to the sovereignty of God is to take form as identifying with others in their joys and sorrows, pointing all the while to God as the sole source of freedom.

Hanson's biblical analysis is extended in the essay by Ronald Sunderland. Sunderland delineates the secular or profane meaning of servitude as a basis for examining the character of servanthood as the term was redefined in the Judeo-Christian tradition. The paradoxical nature of the slave (servant)-master metaphor highlights this redefinition: God's people become slaves, but slaves who are designated chosen sons and daughters whose servanthood is the means by which the freedom and fullness of life are discovered. Thus understood, servanthood, as loving service to fellow members of the community, becomes also a channel by which God's love for the world is revealed. The church is called to emulate the character of servanthood exemplified in the life and work of Jesus, especially by identification with and participation in the plight of broken and oppressed humanity. True servanthood properly expresses this character. In addition, it exists as a sign to the world that God invites all humanity to share in the fullness of life made possible by faith.

Tom Driver, writing in a prophetic voice, explores love and justice in relation to servanthood. He advances and defends the thesis that pastoral ministry properly has no other object or obligation except to be in the service of justice. In Driver's opinion, all other pastoral tasks are authenticated by their contribution to the establishment of justice. The church does not exist "in the world," but on the threshold between the old and new worlds as a prolepsis of the true community in which justice and love are inseparable. Christians are called, accordingly, to be servants of a God whose love is made visible in justice and whose gospel is implemented through devotion to justice. Servants of God are obliged to be involved in public debates concerning the nature and character of a just social order. But in order for this participation and witness to be authentic, the structure and activity of the church itself should be just. In short, Driver argues that God wills justice for creation and that the servant task of pastoral ministry is to work toward the establishment of justice.

James Cone shares Driver's view that servanthood entails being an agent of justice. His defense of this proposition, however, differs from Driver's. Cone argues that the theology of the church has a political, or sociological, component. The presence or absence of this component for Cone is a test of any ecclesiology. If the church is not an agent of justice in society, Cone believes that it ceases to be the church of Jesus Christ. The church's theology is validated by *ministries* that are consistent with the confession that "Jesus is Lord," not by the beauty of its rituals or the artfulness of its creed. Thus, the church is true to its servant calling when it is an agent of justice, expressed by its existence *for* those who are victimized—the "poor" and the "oppressed." Servanthood ought not to be "spiritualized." Rather, it must take concrete form in ministry. When the church expends itself in the pursuit of justice and peace, paradoxically it is vitalized and is what it is meant to be.

Schubert Ogden reminds us that servant ministry must have a theological basis and content. By critically reflecting on the meaning of ministry, defined as the "act of witnessing," the discipline of theology serves the servant task of pastoral ministry. The critical reflection that Ogden considers necessary to servant ministry focuses on both the act of witnessing and the claims explicit and implicit to it. This service of theology to servant ministry, in Ogden's view, ought to occur on academic, professional, and lay levels. It is a task incumbent on every Christian, not only on a few selected people. Only if the content or theological claims inherent to ministry are valid can an act of service be truly characterized as an act of "ministry." Ogden concludes that by validating theological claims about the act and content of ministry, theology indirectly, but essentially, serves servant ministry. In short, the servant task in form and content is validated.

The volume concludes with an essay by Langdon Gilkey in which he considers how the church and its leadership can fulfill their servant tasks in a religiously plural environment. He notes that religious tolerance and ecumenical fellowship have led to a genuine dialogue between religious traditions that formerly were competitors. Like other features of the Christian tradition, servant ministry is subject to reevaluation in a context in which many religions view one another with a degree of mutual respect. Gilkey sees the present environment as an opportunity for the Christian community rather than as a reason for polemics or defensiveness. The opportunity consists in a concern to discover new levels of self-understanding and an effort to discern new ways to serve God in the world. The servant church, in this context, has a responsibility to exercise spiritual leadership, drawing on its rich tradition and wealth of experience to present to congregations "techniques for the development of their spiritual existence." Equally important, in Gilkey's view, is the responsibility of each religious community to prepare its members to live in a world in which a "rough parity" among religions must be faced.

These varied analyses and commentaries provide an intriguing challenge to the contemporary church, its leadership, and its members. Perhaps the message most clearly sounded by each contributor is that the servant task of ministry is more comprehensive and potentially threatening than commonly thought. In short, servanthood entails, for example, more than individual acts of pastoral care, as vitally important as this form of service is in ministry. Three themes seem to weave through the six essays: (1) God is the Sovereign who requires absolute loyalty and obedience despite the presence and lure of false gods. The appropriate human response to the true Master is characterized as servanthood. (2) An element not typically characteristic of the metaphor of master and servant is, in theological perspective, the very basis of the relationship between God and God's people, that is, each freely chooses to be in "bondage" to the other. (3) Authentic servanthood must be expressive of God's love for humanity and God's passion for justice. Critical reflection about the true nature of servanthood and the shape it licitly may have is essential if the church is to be clear about its identity and is to ensure the integrity of its witness to a pluralistic world. The importance of this task for the contemporary church is underscored by a recognition that the world in which it exists is similar to the world of its roots. As in earlier centuries, many powers, ideologies, and belief systems compete for one's loyalty. The question now, as throughout human history, remains, Which master does one serve and what form ought that service take?

The Pastor as Servant

CHAPTER 1

The Servant Dimension of Pastoral Ministry in Biblical Perspective

Paul D. Hanson

"SERVANT" . . . WHAT AN UNUSUAL TERM TO APPLY TO A
profession! One may mitigate its offensiveness by romanticiz-
ing the life of the servant, but the historical meaning and the
existential impact of the term both militate against this temptation. The historical meaning of the terms *'ebed* and *doulos* in
the Old and New Testaments is more accurately translated as
"slave." Described was one whose individual rights were
taken away and whose duty it had become to substitute the
will of his or her master for his or her own. Whether by
military subjugation, indebtedness, or the accident of birth,
the life of the average slave in Hebrew or Greek society was
anything but romantic or enviable.

For the Hebrews, the bondage of slavery was remembered
as the nadir point of their historical existence. It was precisely
by being delivered from the house of bondage, Egypt, that
they were able to become a people with hope and a future. As

Paul D. Hanson, Ph.D., is Busey Professor of Divinity, Divinity School of
Harvard University, Cambridge, Massachusetts.

for the Greek world within which Christianity was born, slavery was the most demeaning of all possible fates. Human dignity was equated with freedom. Slavery stripped a person of human dignity.

One of the great paradoxes of the Bible is that this attitude toward slavery notwithstanding, the faithful of Israel applied to themselves as a title of honor "Servants of Yahweh." In fact, this title was conferred on the most revered of Israel's leaders, including Abraham (Psalm 105:42), Jacob (Ezekiel 37:25), Moses (Exodus 14:31; Numbers 12:7), Joshua (Joshua 24:29), David (2 Samuel 3:18; Psalm 86:2), Elijah (2 Kings 9:36), Zerubbabel (Haggai 2:23; Zecharaiah 3:8ff), and the prophets as a group (2 Kings 17:23). And in Second Isaiah, when a term was needed to designate Israel as Yahweh's agent of salvation, the term chosen was again "servant" (Isaiah 48:20; 49:5f.). Similarly, in the New Testament, Christ was described as appearing on earth in the form of a "servant" (Philippians 2:7), even as the disciples were called the "servants" of their sisters and brothers in faith (2 Corinthians 4:5), "servants of God" (Acts 4:29; Titus 1:1; Revelation 1:1), and "servants of Christ" (Romans 1:1; Galatians 1:10; Colossians 4:12; Revelation 22:3).

The Perspective of the Hebrew Bible

To understand this usage, we must turn to the customs of the ancient Near East, where those in the service of the king were called "servant" or "slave," including those in the highest positions of authority. In treaty documents, vassal kings also go to great lengths to explain that they are faithful servants of the suzerain. This usage extends on into the Hebrew Bible, where David is designated as the servant of Saul (1 Samuel 19:4) and Ahaz, the servant of Tiglath-pileser III as the result of the treaty he had signed with that Assyrian king (2 Kings 16:7).

The treaty concept reflected in such usage permeates Israel's understanding of its relationship with Yahweh. And in this connection it is particularly important to note the exclusivity clause that was a central feature of the ancient Near Eastern treaties.[1] The vassal, in swearing allegiance to the sovereign, was permitted to give his allegiance to no other master. To do so was to court disaster, the belief being that if the harmony assured by the treaty were violated by infidelity, social, and even cosmic, chaos would result.

This political concept provided the background for the religious use of the term servant in the Hebrew Bible. The writers of early Israel described a situation in which many different gods beckoned for the allegiance of the people. The book of Judges, for example, is filled with the struggles within Israel with the many gods. In Judges 10:6 it says:

> And the people of Israel again did what was evil in the sight of [Yahweh], and served the Baals and the Ashtaroth, the gods of Syria, the gods of Sidon, the gods of Moab, the gods of the Ammonites, and the gods of the Philistines; and they forsook [Yahweh], and did not serve [Yahweh].

This passage, together with many others in the Hebrew Bible, presents a world populated with gods, all seeking to claim the heart of the people. But in their every overture those who were true to the ancestral faith recognized the specter of death. And thus, the faithful of Israel, such as the prophets of Yahweh, warned the people repeatedly that however attractive these gods appeared on the surface, following them led to death. Isaiah, for example, closely observed the degeneration of the people that resulted from this apostasy and noted that it culminated in a state of consciousness that so totally perverted the morality of the people that they no longer saw the error of their ways, but felt smugly confident in their perversion:

> We have made a covenant with death,
>   and with Sheol we have an agreement;
> when the overwhelming scourge passes through
>   it will not come to us;

5

> for we have made lies our refuge,
>> and in falsehood we have taken shelter. (Isa. 28:15)

In contrast to such headstrong self-assertiveness, Isaiah pointed to a less dazzling, but utterly dependable orientation:

> In returning and rest you shall be saved;
> in quietness and in trust shall be your strength. (Isa. 30:15)

Only by orienting life toward the true Sovereign could the deadly snares of idolatry in its many forms be avoided. The first commandment was then not merely a tool that Israel had developed to fight against rival cults. It grew out of an awareness that life could be placed on a sure foundation only if life's Center was acknowledged and revered: "Hear, O Israel: The Lord our God is one Lord; and you shall love the Lord your God with all your heart, and with all your soul, and with all your might [Deut. 6:4–5]." When life was considered on its most fundamental level, it therefore revolved on the issue of true and false worship.

We can see clearly that within the Yahwistic view of reality, it was not a matter of *whether* an individual or a community would serve a master or not, but rather a matter of *which* master it would choose. And the choice was no less than a matter of life or death, for only one God was capable of blessing humanity with all that enhances and sustains life. This is stated with clarity and power in Deuteronomy:

> See, I have set before you this day life and good, death and evil. If you obey the commandments of [Yahweh] your God which I command you this day, by loving [Yahweh] your God, by walking in [Yahweh's] ways, and by keeping [Yahweh's] commandments and . . . statutes and . . . ordinances, then you shall live and multiply, and [Yahweh] your God will bless you in the land which you are entering to take possession of it. But if your heart turns away, and you will not hear, but are drawn away to worship other gods and serve them, I declare to you this day, that you shall perish; you shall not live long in the land which you are going over the Jordan to enter and possess.

6

I call heaven and earth to witness against you this day, that I
have set before you life and death, blessing and curse; therefore choose life, that you and your descendants may live,
loving [Yahweh] your God, obeying [Yahweh's] voice, and
cleaving to [Yahweh]. (Deut. 30:15–20)

We begin to see the biblical resolution of the paradox.
Abhorring the type of slavery that was suffered in Egypt and
submitting willingly to Yahweh as servants did not involve a
contradiction, but exposed two sides of one unified view of
life. To submit to the sovereignty of Yahweh was to be drawn
into the orbit of what, in the Hebrew Bible, is called *shalom*,
that is, the harmony of a fully integrated, life-enhancing community of faith and love, which harmony extended outward to
embrace the entire created order. To belong to that community, however, meant assent and commitment; it meant
choosing Yahweh from among the whole wide range of gods in
the world. And that choice was utterly essential to human
well-being, since it entailed being united with the Source of
life rather than with the powers of nothingness and death.
This view of the world is illustrated by the laws dealing with
the release of slaves in Leviticus 25, which ends thus: "For to
me the people of Israel are servants, they are my servants
whom I brought forth out of the land of Egypt: I am [Yahweh]
your God [Lev. 25:55]." What alone gives assurance of not
falling into slavery under the yoke of other mortals? Belonging
to the only Master in whose service true freedom is discovered. Because they are Yahweh's servants, they will neither become enslaved to others nor subject others to the yoke
of slavery.

A fundamental insight into the human situation is found in
these passages, one that lies at the heart of the fulfilled and
blessed life. Although formulated with utter clarity in the first
commandment of the Decalogue and in the *sema' yisra'el* of
Deuteronomy 6, it is so modern as to lie at the center of Paul
Tillich's monumental *Systematic Theology*.[2] In today's world,
as in Israel's, gods lurk on all sides, beckoning for the hearts of

humans. They bear different names and masks, but they still only poorly disguise the death that they bring. Yet even now we see people, often including ourselves, drawn toward materialism, power, loveless sensualism, and nationalism in a misdirected attempt to respond to the longing in the human heart for life. No modern psychologist or theologian has improved on Augustine's poignant description of this basic human situation: "You have made us for yourself, and our heart is restless until it rests in you."[3]

The image of the servant thus may be distasteful to many moderns, as it was to the ancient Greeks, but only because of a faulty understanding of human nature. Relationless human autonomy is a fiction. The human heart simply cannot live in a vacuum. Its longing for love and devotion will force it to cling to a god, to an ultimate loyalty. Happy is the heart that binds itself in devotion to the God who redeems slaves from every bondage and creates for them a community of equality, compassion, and justice. The fundamental vision of the Hebrew Bible was of such a community, united in worship of the one true God and, on the basis of its common ultimate devotion, committed to a solidarity honoring the intrinsic worth of each individual, however weak or lowly. When encountering a human being who is in need, whether through illness, poverty, or oppression, the motivation stirred in the human heart was accordingly clear and derived from the image of the one Sovereign of all who delivered slaves from their bondage and who continued to declare, "If he [or she] cries to me, I will hear, for I am compassionate [Exod. 22:27]."

Unfortunately, the understanding of the paradox of slavery that I have just sketched was by and large the minority position throughout biblical times. In fact, Israel's prophets puzzled over the harsh contradiction between God's persistent initiatives and the people's equally persistent preference for the false gods and concluded that there was a fundamental problem with the human heart, what might be called a predisposition toward apostasy. Jeremiah summarizes this conclusion tersely: "The heart is deceitful above all things, and desperately corrupt; who can understand it? [Jer. 17:9]." The overwhelming evidence from history that humans were predisposed to sin led the prophets to look more deeply at the human predicament and to realize that only a radical new act of God could break this bondage. This led Jeremiah to speak of the day when Yahweh would go beyond the *tora* written on tablets to write God's will on the heart, enabling a situation in which obedience would be born of the individual's devotion to God:

> Behold, the days are coming, says the Lord, when I will make a new covenant with the house of Israel and the house of Judah, not like the covenant which I made with their fathers when I took them by the hand to bring them out of the land of Egypt, my covenant which they broke, though I was their husband, says the Lord. But this is the covenant which I will make with the house of Israel after those days, says the Lord: I will put my law within them, and I will write it upon their hearts; and I will be their God, and they shall be my people. And no longer shall each man teach his neighbor and each his brother, saying "Know the Lord," for they shall all know me, from the least of them to the greatest, says the Lord; for I will forgive their iniquity, and I will remember their sin no more. (Jer. 31:31–34)

Ezekiel similarly looked forward to God's placing a new heart in place of the disobedient one.

> For I will take you from the nations, and gather you from all the countries, and bring you into your own land. I will sprinkle clean water upon you, and you shall be clean from all your uncleannesses, and from all your idols I will cleanse you. A new heart I will give you, and a new spirit I will put within you; and I will take out of your flesh the heart of stone and give you a heart of flesh. And I will put my spirit within you, and cause you to walk in my statutes and be careful to observe my ordinances. (Ezek. 36:24–27)

Second Isaiah went further still and declared that God's act of breaking humans from their bondage to sin could come only through the agency of a servant who would so intimately identify with their bondage as to bear their griefs and carry their sorrows. For in the suffering of this servant of Yahweh, the people would be shocked into recognizing a punishment being borne on their behalf. Here was one willingly taking on himself the bondage belonging to others and offering himself as "an offering for sin":

> Yet it was the will of the Lord to bruise him;
>   he has put him to grief;
> when he makes himself an offering for sin,
>   he shall see his offspring, he shall prolong his days;
> the will of the Lord shall prosper in his hand. (Isa. 53:10)

The mystery of the radical solution to the persistent problem of human slavery to sin found in Isaiah 53 is sublimely deep, and hence not reducible to facile formulas. The integrity of the text is violated if we claim to resolve the problem of whether the servant is an individual or a remnant of Israel. Harm is done to its message if we must decide whether its message was primarily directed toward the exiles or toward generations yet to come. The prophecy of Second Isaiah grows out of the deep yearning of Yahwistic faith for the redemption of a people from their bondage to all false gods and, in sum, to sin. And it boldly declares that redemption would come as the result of God's acting through the Servant, that is, a person or a people so intimately identifying with the bondage of others as to become, in solidarity with sinners, the means of their healing. [4]

The New Testament Perspective

The lines of continuity between the Testaments in regard to the central paradox of the slave/servant image are unmistakable. Paul, for example, portrays the negative side of slavery as

10

passionately as Jeremiah. He speaks of captivity to a "law of sin" and a "body of death":

> So I find it to be a law that when I want to do right, evil lies close at hand. For I delight in the law of God, in my inmost self, but I see in my members another law at war with the law of my mind and making me captive to the law of sin which dwells in my members. Wretched man that I am! Who will deliver me from this body of death? Thanks be to God through Jesus Christ our Lord! So then, I of myself serve the law of God with my mind, but with my flesh I serve the law of sin. (Rom. 7:21–25)

Humans are situated in a world populated by false gods that strain to entangle them in deadly bonds. "So with us; when we were children, we were slaves to the elemental spirits of the universe . . . in bondage to beings that by nature are no gods [Gal. 4:3, 8]." What this precarious situation calls for, according to Paul, is not a heroic declaration by humans that they are henceforth free. Fully in keeping with the realism of the Hebrew Bible, such human acts only assure turning "back again to the weak and beggarly elemental spirits, whose slaves you want to be once more [Gal. 4:9]." For rather than securing freedom, they merely create the "empty room" that is receptive to a host of demons that are more pernicious than those that preceded. The paradox put forward is thus identical to that found in Hebrew scripture:

> Do you not know that if you yield yourselves to any one as obedient slaves, you are slaves of the one whom you obey, either of sin, which leads to death, or of obedience, which leads to righteousness? But thanks be to God, that you who were once slaves of sin have become obedient from the heart to the standard of teaching to which you were committed, and, having been set free from sin, have become slaves of righteousness. (Rom. 6:16–18)

Here, as in the Hebrew Bible, we see the myth of heroic autonomy shattered. Every person, whether knowingly or

11

not, is attached to an ultimate devotion. In the imagery of slavery, "you are slaves of the one whom you obey, either of sin, which leads to death, or of obedience, which leads to righteousness." For Paul, this involves one of the deep mysteries of the heart. The one who has not been redeemed by God through Christ is in the most frightening, life-destructive bondage. As the Gospel of John describes the situation, "every one who commits sin is a slave to sin [John 8:34]." Only one avenue of escape exists, accepting what God has done, the God who sent "his own Son in the likeness of sinful flesh and for sin," and thereby "condemned sin in the flesh [Rom. 8:3]." Of course, acknowledging God as the only one who is capable of redeeming one from the slavery of death and sin involves acknowledging God as one's Sovereign, accepting God's will as one's own, allowing the righteousness of God to take up habitation in one's heart, and thus becoming "obedient from the heart" (cf. Jer. 31:31–34). Paul thus rejoices in the fact that those who were formerly "slaves of sin" had now become "slaves of righteousness." They "belong to another" (Romans 7:4), the One whose service leads not to bondage, but to the true freedom that can be found solely in fellowship with the one true God.

As observed earlier, the late prophets of the Hebrew Bible puzzled over the human predicament, especially the predisposition of humans to repudiate the true God in favor of bondage to false gods. They had concluded that release from bondage depended on a new initiative by God. For Second Isaiah, this involved the mystery of a Servant, who would identify fully with the suffering of the captive people and through whom God would accomplish the redemption of the lost. At the heart of the Christian gospel is the announcement that Christ was the Servant of God who had identified fully with the suffering of the people and through whose suffering, death, and resurrection those bound by sin and death were redeemed. If we are to understand the significance of the biblical image of the servant for ministry, we must recognize the focal point of that image in New Testament Christology.

The repertory of images available to the early church from its Hebrew scriptures, as well as from its larger religious environment, offered many possible ways of explaining divine deliverance from death and sin. But out of these possibilities one commended itself as the most adequate way of understanding what they had experienced in the company of Jesus, that being the image of the "Servant of the Lord." In Jesus, God was seen reaching out to lost humans, affirming solidarity with them, even identifying with their suffering and alienation. God was thus uniquely present in "Christ Jesus, who, though he was in the form of God, did not count equality with God a thing to be grasped, but emptied himself, taking the form of a servant, being born in the likeness of [humans] [Phil. 2:5–6]." The human family, according to this Christology, could be healed neither through human power nor through dazzling theophany, but only through God's agent, the Christ, entering intimately into the experience of humans and becoming one with them in suffering and even death. The Gospel of John presents the same Christology in a simple, but powerful story. The scene was the last supper of Jesus with his disciples before his death. Jesus "rose from supper, laid aside his garments, and girded himself with a towel. Then he poured water into a basin, and began to wash the disciples' feet, and to wipe them with the towel [John 13:4–5]." From this he drew a lesson:

> Do you know what I have done to you? You call me Teacher and Lord; and you are right, for so I am. If I then, your Lord and Teacher, have washed your feet, you also ought to wash one another's feet. For I have given you an example, that you also should do as I have done to you. Truly, truly, I say to you, a servant is not greater than his master; nor is he who is sent greater than [the one] who sent him. If you know these things, blessed are you if you do them. (John 13:12–17)

From the example of God's servant Jesus Christ, the disciples were to learn the secret of the slavery in which was found true freedom. The christological hymn of Philippians 2, from which I quoted, begins thus: "Do nothing from selfishness or conceit, but in humility count others better than yourselves. Let each of you look not only to his own interests, but also to the interests of others. Have this mind among yourselves, which is yours in Christ Jesus [Phil. 2:3–5]." Only in the gathering of those acknowledging no sovereign other than the one true God could genuine freedom be found. For devotion to God freed humans from the devisive, destructive gods that set one human against the other and filled them instead with the loving spirit of service that was genuinely concerned for the welfare of the other. Dietrich Bonhoeffer discovered the paradox of this slavery that frees one to love in the passage, so troubling to many, in which Jesus says, "If any one comes to me and does not hate his own father and mother and wife and children and brothers and sisters, yes, and even his own life, he cannot be my disciple [Luke 14:26]." On the surface this seems harsh. We want to reject it as heartless and rush out to affirm our love for others directly. But Bonhoeffer points out that when we move out in the manner of the hero to love others under the delusion that we are free agents, our love becomes a disguise for efforts to control the other. The only love that affirms the freedom of the other is the love that is mediated by Christ, for the love that arises out of our submitting to Christ, and thereby being freed from our need to control and dominate, is alone pure.

> Since the coming of Christ, his followers have no more imme-
> diate realities of their own, not in their family relationships nor
> in the ties with their nation nor in the relationships formed in
> the process of living. Between father and son, husband and
> wife, the individual and the nation, stands Christ the Medi-
> ator, whether they are able to recognize him or not. We cannot
> establish direct contact outside ourselves except through him,
> through his word, and through our following of him. To think
> otherwise is to deceive ourselves.[5]

For example, in loving our parents, wives, children, colleagues, friends, and even those who cause us grief, when that

14

love is channeled through Christ, an alternative community takes root within the God-given freedom to identify with the other that has its source in God's love and in the love of the servant Christ. As Jesus taught his disciples:

> You know that those who are supposed to rule over the Gentiles lord it over them, and their great men exercise authority over them. But it shall not be so among you; but whoever would be great among you must be your servant, and whoever would be first among you must be slave of all. (Mark 10:42–45)

I believe that true spiritual formation among Christians is impossible without an unambiguous affirmation of this biblical understanding of our slavery under God and the resulting relationship whereby we relate to all other realities through our primary devotion to God. All other forms of relating inevitably degenerate into exploitation for the simple reason that if we are not slaves of God, other masters claim our hearts. Only if we are clear regarding our primary life devotion can our understanding of our vocations be clarified. No longer drifting between penultimate devotions, and thus lost, we have been brought home; as Paul explains, "we are children of God, and if children, then heirs, heirs of God and fellow heirs with Christ, provided we suffer with him in order that we may also be glorified with him [Rom. 8:16–17]." This then is the life characterized by the "mind . . . which you have in Christ Jesus," a life prepared to empathize and to suffer by a love that unites all those loved by God in a sense of faithful solidarity.

The Biblical Image of Servant and Pastoral Ministry Today

Our brief sketch of the image of the servant in the Hebrew Bible and the New Testament provides us with the background to ask, "What contribution does this image make to our understanding of ministry today?"[6] We must realize that the abolition of the institution of slavery in our society has not eliminated the frightening connotations associated with the concept of slavery. Many forms of bondage weigh on people today, including meaningless vocations, social and economic structures that discriminate against minorities and women, hopelessness in the face of the nuclear threat, not to mention the ravaging power of perennial demons like poverty, hunger, addiction, materialism, and promiscuity. If we add to this a climate within which cults of personal self-fulfillment and blatant narcissism are at a high point, we can understand why so many people are loath to apply the image of servant to their vocational identity.

Ministers, as a group, have their own reasons to reinforce this reluctance. In a pluralistic society within which the very vocation of the ministry is questionable to many, the image of servant, or, worse yet, slave, threatens to erode further an already weakened aura of authority. Beyond this, ministers are not immune, being human after all, to the status consciousness and accompanying materialism that has swept over the professional world as a whole. How can ministers maintain their self-respect among successful lawyers, climbing business executives, and wealthy medical doctors if they lag behind on the ladder of progress as ones called "not to be served but to serve."

Rather than have their morale dragged down even lower, it is time for the ministerial profession to speak out. Our society is in a brittle state precisely because the grace of serving others has been so severely defined out of the modern world view. The biblical language may have an archaic ring, and hence may be in need of reformulation, but in this context we can still use it in describing a society that is being assailed by a host of false gods and in which many have attached their hearts to these gods. Consider the priorities of a nation with our economic strength and yet with millions of hungry citizens. Consider our shameful, wasteful indulgence within a world plagued by starvation.

If we seek to apply the image of servant or slave, we must first recognize that the human situation is predominantly one of bondage, the many social and personal forms of which need not be enumerated here. More important than identification of the forms of bondage is clear recognition of the agents of deliverance. The candidates are myriad. Some are ideologies that promise the good life to those who pledge their allegiance. Some are leaders who promise a new prosperity predicated on military might and economic superiority. One looks long among them to find a protagonist appealing to anything other than human selfishness.

To such a world Second Isaiah still points to an arresting alternative by describing a vastly different type of agent: "Surely he has borne our griefs and carried our sorrows [Isa. 53:4]." In such a world the Gospel of John still offers a basis for hope in portraying the Master washing the feet of his friends. Within such a world the apostle Paul reminds a faithful, but wavering community: "For you were called to freedom [brothers and sisters]; only do not use your freedom as an opportunity for the flesh, but through love be servants of one another [Gal. 5:13]."

We must face the modern situation honestly. The biblical image of servant is not popular. In the face of much bondage, much sickness, and much sorrow, there are many professionals who are eager to offer their services for a dear price and from the protection of a status lifted far above those served. "You know that those who are supposed to rule over the Gentiles lord it over them [Mark 10:42]." But is there still a place for the servant?

I fear that if there is not, our lofty civilization will swiftly degenerate. The social and economic proofs seem too powerful to deny. Ministers alone are not going to reverse this trend. But there is hope that their alternative concept of vocation may keep alive and even revive a true sense of deliverance from bondage within the freedom that prevails where God's sovereignty is acknowledged.

According to that alternative concept of vocation, agents of healing and deliverance are those who do not lord it over others, but identify with others in their joys and sorrows, successes and losses, recoveries and setbacks. But we have learned from our biblical heritage that such identification, and servanthood, does not grow out of heroic decisions, but out of personal deliverance from false gods and integration into the community finding true freedom in acknowledgment of the sole Sovereignty of God. The hero reaches down to save and further demeans the one in bonds. The servant of Christ experiences his or her solidarity with the one in bondage, a solidarity based on the awareness of God's love embracing both.[7]

I have been describing a vocation that cannot be learned in graduate schools or in professional societies. For at the heart of such a vocational understanding is a freedom from the self-centered motivations that usually underlie professional choices and decisions. This freedom exists in the life of one whose needs for status and recognition are satisfied by the deep sense of being accepted and sustained by a gracious God. If the life of a servant is cut off from the renewal of this sense that comes through worship and communal celebration, a life line is severed and confusion is sure to result. That this involves a lifelong commitment to worship, study, and reflection is undeniable, for as I have observed, the model of servanthood is not popular in the dominant culture today. Commonly, we will find the sources of renewal in the classics of our religious heritage, both in scripture and in tradition. In a recent lecture, James Luther Adams offered this illustration of those centering symbols that give expression to the transcendent point of reference that preserves our ultimate grounding, our freedom, and our sense of solidarity with all humans:

> I am thinking of Albrecht Durer's 1507 picture of "The Praying Hands." The praying hands point to the source of being and meaning beyond all creatures. As Boswell's Johnson would say, these hands express more than wonder; they express awe before the divine Majesty. Or as Augustine would say, they

warn us against giving to any creature the love that belongs alone to the Creator, whether that creature be a liturgical formula, an institution, or a document. Each of these creatures may point to the ultimate ground, but none can exhaust or define its bounds. It cannot be spatialized. Vocation is then from a formative and transformative power that is sovereign and is the enemy of idolatry whether it be religious, ecclesiastical, cultural, or secular.[8]

While not denying that such an alternative concept of vocation may place one in a position that, by human standards, is lonely, both our long confessional heritage and our contemporary spiritual homes provide us with an empowering vision. Wherever our identification with "one of the least of these, my brothers or sisters" occurs, it occurs not as an isolated human act, but as a rivulet in the vast stream flowing at the heart of all creation that is actively healing the wounded, freeing the enslaved, and preparing for a great banquet in which all God's people will be free. That vision, which we glimpse in worship and for which we yearn in the prayer Jesus taught, is a gift of God's Spirit. It can give God's servants the grace and power to acknowledge the depth of human bondage and the dearth of loving servants and yet enter the fray with courage and energy, knowing that where a human servant acknowledges her or his solidarity with a human in need through an act of loving service, God is present, and God's realm is coming.[9]

CHAPTER 2

The Character of Servanthood

Ronald H. Sunderland

IN THE POST-SIXTIES ERA IT APPEARS THAT, IN CONTRAST TO their immediate predecessors, the first concern of today's undergraduates is their preparation for a successful business career. In this climate, industry, creativity, ambition, and other achievement-oriented traits are likely to relegate the notion of servanthood to an insignificant place, if it is considered at all. Indeed, servanthood has been debased to such a degree that it is usually deemed antithetical to those ideals customarily associated with "success." The term is more likely to be perceived in a pejorative manner, in the sense of servitude. It is to this concept that attention is first directed. The roots of slavery as servitude in the secular or profane use will be examined as a basis for exploring the reconceptualization of the term slave in the Judeo-Christian scriptures. The extent to which servanthood is a valid model for the role of the church as the people of God is explored in the final section.

Ronald H. Sunderland, Ed.D., is Research Fellow, Institute of Religion, Houston, Texas.

Slavery in Antiquity

The generic term slave used by ancient cultures and our own is the source from which other designations of servitude have been derived. The varied scope of the construct is indicated by a review of some of the words that have found their way into the English language: slave, fief, serf, vassal, chattel, churl, liege, flunky, menial, bondman/woman, drudge, subject, and servant. The word slave is of special concern to this essay, since it translates the two terms, *'ebed* and *doulos*, that dominate both the secular and religious uses to which the discussion must be directed.

Slavery is one of the oldest, and has proved one of the most enduring, of societal practices. It can be traced to the most primitive cultures and was accepted universally as the price of defeat. From the earliest tribal conflicts to subtler forms of oppression that have persisted into our own era, conquest usually has been accompanied by enslavement of the conquered. Not infrequently, entire ethnic groups were enslaved as a result of war. Slavery often resulted from slave raids but might also issue from failure to discharge a debt to a landholder. The term slave, applied to all these uses, implies a servitude enforced by a superior on an inferior who presumably did not accept the status voluntarily —a status that could only be changed by the will of the victor or master.

The Greeks justified slavery by attributing master-status to victors and subject-status to the vanquished. Heraclitus (ca. 500 B.C.E.) appears to have been the first to reflect on the differences that separated humans from one another. He stated that "war, the father and king" of all things and beings, "proved some to be gods, others to be men: some he has made slaves, others he has made freemen."[1] The slaves and their descendants were prisoners; their conquerors and rulers were the freemen. But this attitude toward slaves and enslavement was not universal. Socrates foreshadowed a more enlightened and humane influence toward the poor and the oppressed. He

21

not only refrained from the contempt for the underprivileged later manifested by Plato and Aristotle, but also protested the prejudice against those who had been forced into servitude.

Plato (427–347 B.C.E.) compared the slave to the human body; the master was the body's soul. Artisans, farmers, mechanics, small traders, and the like were reduced to virtual servitude, functioning in a state of wardship appropriate to the masses in Plato's *Republic*. Below these classes, the truly menial tasks of the community were to be performed by slaves who were destitute of any rights except protection from brutal treatment by their masters. Callicles, Plato's mouthpiece in the dialogue *Gorgias*, refers to the dominion that the strong exercise over the weak as a fact of "natural law," or "natural justice."[2]

Aristotle (384–322 B.C.E.) identified the taking of slaves as "among the varieties of the chase," as illustrated by the enslavement of Phaedo of Ellis, a man of noble birth who was enslaved as a prisoner of war and transported to Athens, where he was later redeemed by Socrates. Enslavement was not only not a cause for protest, but it was also seen as the appointed lot of those "who are designed by Nature to serve, and who resist this their destination."[3] Thus, Aristotle discounted the perception of slavery as merely the result of arbitrary conventions. He searched for a rational defense of slavery, justifying it, in accordance with "natural law," in the interests of the slaves, who were unfit to govern themselves.

Slavery, according to this view, was counted a blessing, since the needs of the enslaved could best be met in this station. Aristotle argued that slaves could not exercise any will or interests of their own: they were merely tools or instruments, an extension of their masters' physical nature. This attitude sanctioned the owners' exploitation of human nature, reducing the character of slavery to "dependence, disability, powerlessness, sinfulness, and negation of autonomous self-dependence."[4]

Yet the legitimacy of slavery had been questioned before

Aristotle. The poet Euripedes (480–406 B.C.E.), a great Greek dramatist, protested the practice of slavery and rejected it as a human device, rather than endemic to the "natural" state of humankind. He courageously attacked this pillar of society and the theory on which it was based, holding that, "beyond the name, there is no difference in nature, but only in convention, between bond and free. . . . In the heart of the serf there often beats a nobler heart than in that of his master."[5]

Perceiving the contradictions, Aristotle dramatized them in a dialogue between the advocates of slavery and those of human rights. The latter protest that mere superiority of power should not suffice to justify the theft of liberty. Aristotle identified two types of slavery: a "natural" slavery arising from the subordination of the inferior to the superior and that arising from convention, for example, from war. Under pressure, the proponents of slavery appeal to the "intention" of Nature to distinguish by external marks those who were fitted for menial tasks and those who were capable of better things. This argument broke down when it proved difficult to "unfallibly and unambiguously separate those destined by Nature to slavery from those appointed to freedom." The conclusive argument, to Aristotle, was the arbitrary: "Let the alien serve the Hellene: they are bondmen, we are free," which reduces to, "barbarism and slavedom are by nature identical."[6] To the Greeks, such bondage was "part of the cosmic hierarchy, of the divine scheme for ordering and governing the forces of evil and rebellion," on the one hand and, on the other, an acknowledgment that "all men" are *not* created equal, since "from the moment of their birth, some men are marked out for subjection, others for rule."[7]

The metaphysical assumption that some beings were destined to be slaves by their subordinate natures underlies the world views of both Plato and Aristotle. The perception that such inequality was mandated by the human condition provided a rationale for the practice of enforced servitude that has characterized most societies. It not only served the privileged classes of Greek and Roman societies as a rational basis for slavery, but was also adopted by the Western world, with strong theological underpinnings, as a rationalization that was seldom challenged until the nineteenth century, and, indeed, survives in the twentieth, albeit in subtler forms of oppression and control.

The very inequality that separated master and slave, however, also paradoxically served to bind each to the other. The most virtuous slave was the one who fulfilled completely his or her assigned service, conforming to the master's expectations. This linkage draws attention to a feature that is implicit in any discussion of the character of servitude: the contradiction inherent in the relationship that D.B. Davis identified as the "problem" of slavery. Paraphrasing Hegel, he suggested that the identity of the master depends on having a slave who recognizes him as such. Hegel had argued that, whereas the master is "consciousness that exists only *for itself*," his "lordship" is contingent on the bonded-one's seemingly unessential consciousness and the actions that issue from it.[8] On the surface it seems that the master's independence and autonomy would indicate the absence of any "need" for the slave, whose very existence has become totally dependent on the master's every whim and whose essence is life or existence for the other. This led Hegel to state that the actions of the slave are thus properly actions on the part of the master. He concluded that, since the slave is essential to the concept of mastery, the more perfect the slave, the more enslaved becomes the master!

Hegel stated that one understands bondage only in relation to lordship. If this interpretation is valid, then one is forced to use what Jürgen Moltmann terms a dialectical principle of knowledge, which he delineates in the words of the German philosopher F.W. Schelling: "Every being can be revealed only in its opposite. Love only in hatred, unity only in conflict."[9] Applied to our subject, the character of servanthood as slavery is thus defined in relation to the freedom that is denied to the enslaved, the autonomy that is stolen, and the forfeiting of one's labor, since that labor is required of the slave by the master, to whom the fruits belong. If this principle holds, it follows that any radical redefinition of the meaning of "lordship" would entail a similarly radical change in the concept of slavery and the nature of the master-servant relationship. Just such a shift occurred with respect to the relationship of Israel with God. Before turning to the Jewish scriptures, however, a postscript should be added.

The bonding of the master and slave inherent to the relationship assumes the form of a contract, albeit one that is hardly mutual, being enforced by the stronger on the weaker. There are obvious elements of authority, responsibility, and accountability required of slaves by their owners and, in some states—for example, in Roman law—required of owners toward their slaves. One element of this contractual form is of particular interest to this discussion. Even when circumstances provided for the termination of service, due to the fulfillment of commitments or the generosity of the master, a slave might voluntarily surrender the right to freedom and choose to remain in servitude. Such provisions emphasize the symbiotic nature of the relationship. The dependency and continuation of slave status were compensated by the provision of accommodation and security as a member of the owner's household. The voluntary adoption of slave status was marked by a public event, as in Hebrew society, in which provision was made in the Law for voluntary enslavement (e.g., Exodus 21:5–6; Leviticus 25:39ff; Deuteronomy 15:16–17). The passage from Exodus describes the public announcement, at the doorpost of the house, when the slave's ear was pierced by an awl and the person became "slave for life." The Deuteronomic reference tells of a slave who, because he loved his master and fared well with him, also chose servitude for life.

Redefinition of the Term Slave in the Judeo-Christian Scriptures

The Jewish Scriptures

The earliest biblical reference to slavery in the profane sense is found in the Torah. Noah condemned Ham's son, Canaan, to be the "slave of slaves" to Shem and Japheth (Genesis 9:25–27). Abram's offering of Sarah to Pharaoh was accompanied by his growing wealth, including the acquisition of male and female slaves. Abimelech's blessing of Abraham when he returned Sarah to her husband was sealed with the gift of sheep and cattle, and male and female slaves to Abraham (Genesis 20:14; see also Leviticus 25:46).

The Jewish legal system discriminated between two classes of servitude—the servanthood of Jews and that of Gentiles. Within these categories, the Torah further differentiated two classes of Hebrew slaves: those who willingly sold themselves into servitude and those whom the courts sold for the failure to make good a theft. In each case, the law enjoined masters from ill treatment, that is, the treatment of Hebrew servants as *slaves*, a term that was confined to Gentiles, who could be bought and sold and who, with their descendants, were regarded as property. Nevertheless, even bondservants—slaves—came under the protection of Jewish law, which limited the absolute power of the master.

Hebrew servants contracted to landowners as bondsmen were to be freed in the year of jubilee: "You shall not use him to work for you as a slave *['ebed]*. His status shall be that of a hired man *[shakir]*. . . . Because they are my slaves whom I brought out of Egypt, they shall not be sold as slaves are sold [Lev. 25:39–43, NEB]." (See also Exodus 20:2; Deuteronomy 5:6, 15; 6:21.) The prophet Jeremiah denounced the permanent enslavement of Hebrews by Jewish masters as the gravest of sins (34:8–24), an offense for which the kingdom of Judah had forfeited any claim on God's mercy.

The transition of the understanding of the slave-lord relationship from a secular to a religious motif was not exclusive to Hebrew religion but reached its highest expression in the "servant of God" figure in the Old Testament and Jesus as the Servant-king in the New Testament. The common starting point is the sense of belonging that was fundamental to the Hebrew *'ebed* and the Greek *doulos.* In both secular and religious uses the slave belonged to another. In Deuteronomy 15:15; 20:2, for example, the Israelites were reminded that they had been slaves in Egypt, "and the Lord your God redeemed you." But the people of Israel had been redeemed from slave owners in Egypt to become slaves to God. The term *'ebed* signifies the humble self-expression of the pious in the presence of God. Walter Zimmerli notes that

> just as the inferior, in speaking to the superior, refers to himself humbly as "thy servant" in the third person, this manner of speech is all the more appropriate when a man stands in the presence of God. . . . He who confesses allegiance to a master withdraws himself from the dominion of all other possible masters, and so with inner justification can request the master whose allegiance he owns to be careful on his part to preserve his power and to protect his servant (see II Kings 6:7).[10]

He suggests that in this sort of situation, the Lord's honor is at stake. If by this supplication, "I am thy servant and thy son: come up, and save me," the servant's own performance is stressed, then the self-description *['ebed]* acquires a strongly active tone. If, however, "the already experienced favor of God is emphasized, then the name *['ebed]* marks the attitude of thankful self-surrender."[11] Indeed, the secular practice of piercing a slave's ear to signify lifelong servitude became the powerful metaphor for one's lifelong commitment ("surrender") to the service of God. But now it was a voluntary act: "Sacrifice and offering thou didst not desire; mine ears hast thou opened: . . . I delight to do thy will, O my God: yea, thy law *is* within my heart [Ps. 40:6, 8, KJV]." (See also Jeremiah 31:31ff.)

The servants of God exist in a contractual (covenant) relationship to their Lord, who assigns their work and to whom they are accountable for the proper discharge of their service. In the Hebrew Bible the image of servanthood reached its fulfillment in the figure of the servant of the Lord, who fulfills the divine mission, not only to Israel, but to the world, which is the object of God's love. But the servant relationship now offered by God to Israel was not couched in menial terms. Israel was portrayed as God's favored child, with whom the Lord established a new covenant, written in the peoples' hearts (Jeremiah 31:31). As God planted Israel as a vine that God tended, so God chose and adopted Israel as "son." Moses was instructed to address this claim to Pharaoh, the slave owner who must surrender the slaves to their rightful Lord, who has given them a new status: "Israel is my first-born son. I have told you to let my son go, so that he may worship me [Exod. 4:23, NEB]." God chooses—adopts—Israel, who in turn must choose whether to live in this relationship in a servant status that differs radically from that of other slaves on whom servitude has been forced. Such servanthood is to be marked by love for the Lord's ways, fidelity, trust, commitment to justice, and compassion for others who are in need— especially for the oppressed who cannot defend themselves and who do not have anyone to speak for them. The character of servanthood is clear: the central notion of belonging is stated, yet the relationship is one born out of choice. Israel must choose whether to live as "slave for life."

The servanthood into which Israel was invited to enter was to be marked by the commitment to love the Lord their God with all their heart and mind and soul and strength. It was not a servitude demanded of them and enforced by power but was to be the free response of sons and daughters whose love for the parent was "written in their hearts," that is, arose out of the very essence of their beings. Their fidelity should be their glad response to the Lord's discipline, which was not harsh like that of a slave lord, but the gentle reproof of a lover in whose company they gladly chose to walk (Proverbs 3:12, also Deuteronomy 8:1–6; Isaiah 2:3, 5; Hosea 11:10). But choose they must.

The choice is seldom clearer or more stark than in Moses' charge to the people about to cross Jordan:

> The commandment that I lay on you this day is not too difficult for you, it is not too remote. It is not in heaven, that you should say, "Who will go up to heaven for us to fetch it and tell it to us, so that we can keep it?" Nor is it beyond the sea, that you should say, "Who will cross the sea for us to fetch it and tell it to us, so that we can keep it?" It is a thing very near to you, upon your lips and in your heart ready to be kept.
>
> Today I offer you the choice of life and good, or death and evil. If you obey the commandments of the Lord your God which I give you this day, by loving the Lord your God, by conforming to his ways and by keeping his commandments, statutes, and laws, then you will live and increase, and the Lord your God will bless you in the land which you are entering to occupy. But if your heart turns away and you do not listen and you are led on to bow down to other gods and worship them, I tell you this day that you will perish; you will not live long in the land which you will enter to occupy after crossing the Jordan. I summon heaven and earth to witness against you this day: I offer you the choice of life or death, blessing or curse. Choose life and then you and your descendants will live: love the Lord your God, obey him and hold fast to him: that is life for you and length of days in the land which the Lord swore to give to your forefathers, Abraham, Isaac and Jacob. (Deut. 30:11–20, NEB)

Joshua would later place the same choice before the people: "Hold the Lord in awe then, and worship him in loyalty and truth. Banish the gods whom your fathers worshipped beside the Euphrates and in Egypt, and worship the Lord. But if it does not please you to worship the Lord, choose here and now whom you will worship: the gods whom your forefathers worshipped beside the Euphrates, or the gods of the Amorites in whose land you are living. But I and my family, we will worship the Lord [Josh. 24:14–16, NEB]."

The character of servanthood is delineated in sharp and unambiguous terms: The Lord's servants shall put their trust in Yahweh because they know that only from God can they draw strength and endure (Psalms 18, 19, 29, 43, etc.) and that the God who promises is faithful (Psalms 5, 7, 31; also Isaiah 26:4 and Jeremiah 7:4). Truth shall be on their lips, and they will be committed to justice, remembering that the Lord has dealt justly with them. Love of justice is always linked to love of righteousness: "Let justice roll on like a river and righteousness like an everflowing stream [Amos 5:24, NEB]." (See also Micah 6:8.) As God's justice is always tempered with mercy, God's servants who have known compassion shall show compassion toward others. The care of the oppressed and the helpless (the orphan, the widow, or the stranger) shall be their special responsibility; they must never forget that they had been orphans and strangers in Egypt, where they had received comfort from their Lord. Servants to whom the Lord has spoken tenderly shall humble themselves, in the knowledge that their Lord dwells with those who are broken and humble in spirit, "to revive the spirit of the humble, to revive the courage of the broken [Isa. 57:15, NEB]."

The Christian Scriptures

The characteristics of servanthood found in the Old Testament were carried over by Christian authors in the New Testament, where, at each point, the images were sharpened. The nearest Greek equivalent to the Hebrew 'ebed is duolos, the technical term for "one born a slave." There was not only no drawing back from the term in the early church; it was claimed vigorously as a symbol of honor to be a slave of Christ, since Christ himself had assumed "the form of a slave [Phil. 2:7]."

Jesus identified the character of servanthood that was to be the mark of his fellow servants (cf. *sun-doulos*, Colossians 4:7) in two instances, Mark 10:41–45 and Luke 22:24–27. The setting of the Marcan passage is the departure of Jesus with the disciples from Caesarea Philippi. The third prediction of the passion (Mark 10:32–34) is followed by the request of James and John to sit with him in the places of honor in his kingdom. The arguments generated among the disciples drew a sharp response attributed by Mark to Jesus:

> When the other ten heard this, they were indignant with James and John. Jesus called them to him and said, "You know that in the world the recognized rulers lord it over their subjects, and their great men make them feel the weight of authority. That is not the way with you; among you, whoever wants to be great must be your servant, and whoever wants to be first must be the willing slave of all. For even the Son of Man did not come to be served but to serve, and to give up his life as a ransom for many." (Mark 10:41–45, NEB)

Luke sets the parallel saying in the upper room, when, at supper, they disputed which of them should rank the highest:

> Then a jealous dispute broke out: who among them should rank the highest? But he said, "In the world, kings lord it over their subjects; and those in authority are called their country's 'Benefactors.' Not so with you: on the contrary, the highest among you must bear himself like the youngest, the chief of you like a servant. For who is greater—the one who sits at table or the servant who waits on him? Surely the one who sits at table. Yet here I am among you like a servant." (Luke 22:24–27, NEB)

On both occasions the rebuke serves to establish the character of servanthood. Again, it was defined by contrasting it with what it was not! The "servant of the Lord" is now to be identified as one who deliberately rejects the superior status and power manifested by the recognized rulers of the world, choosing instead the role of a slave,[12] which Jesus had modeled for them.

Paul especially did not hesitate to identify himself as a slave of Christ, nor to identify other believers as his fellow slaves. The relationship was confirmed by the use of the language of sacrifice: they had been bought with a price (1 Corinthians 6:20; 7:23), so they belonged to Christ. Yet now the term slave has a new nuance. Through the act of redemption they became slaves who are recognized as *sons and daughters* (Galatians 4:7). Paul does not apologize for this mixing of metaphors; it must be assumed that he wanted his listeners to struggle with the apparent contradiction without losing the force of either image. The two concepts are not mutually exclusive; indeed, the use of the two images heightens the effect of each. It is through sharing in the servant nature embodied by Christ that his fellow servants become heirs with him to God's promises (Galatians 3:29; Titus 3:7; Hebrews 6:17). But to share in the nature of Christ means to share in his work. In the first instance, that is the "work" of loving one another as fellow slaves and joint heirs (1 John 4:7–12; see also John 13:34–35).

The image "a slave of God" was to characterize their relationship with one another; they were to be slaves to one another in love (Galatians 5:13). Nowhere is this service to one another more powerfully presented than in the washing of the disciples' feet, which John substitutes for the institution of the Lord's Supper. D. Moody Smith has noted that the Fourth Gospel does not present Jesus as performing a ministry, or ministering—that is, the words *diakonein, diakonia* do not appear. This absence would seem to suit John's high Christology, but in fact, the image of servanthood is presented through the humblest ministry of service (John 13:1–17). Smith identifies Luke 22:25–27 as a possible link between the Synoptics and John, with respect to John's characterization of servanthood/slavery. In the Lucan saying the institution of the Lord's Supper is followed by a "kind of brief farewell discourse" in which Jesus speaks of ministering or serving (in terms similar to those of Mark 10:45): "The kings of the

Gentiles exercise lordship over them. . . . But not so with you; . . . let . . . the leader [be] as one who serves."[13]

The importance for us is found in the closing image of the pericope:

> After washing their feet and taking his garments again, he sat down. "Do you understand what I have done for you?" he asked. "You call me 'Master' and 'Lord,' and rightly so, for that is what I am. Then if I, your Lord and Master, have washed your feet, you also ought to wash one another's feet. I have set you an example: you are to do as I have done for you. In very truth I tell you, a servant is not greater than his master, nor a messenger than the one who sent him. If you know this, happy are you if you act upon it." (John 13:12–17, NEB)

Having quite literally assumed the role of a slave, Jesus' action dramatized the moral demand implicit in his action. He established the character of servanthood by directing the disciples and their successors to think of themselves as *douloō* to one another. It became a role that they were to assume with joy and thanksgiving in response to the proclamation of the good news of God's love. Theirs was to be the response of those who had been reminded that they, too, had once been slaves to other masters but had now been redeemed by a loving Lord (cf. Deuteronomy 15:15).

The Johannine stress on the building up of the Christian community as a first responsibility of the members of that community is implied throughout the Gospels and is explicit in the epistles. The Letter to the Ephesians emphasizes that our work is to "grow up into Christ. He is the head, and on him the whole body depends. Bonded and knit together by every constituent joint, the whole frame grows through the due activity of each part, and builds itself up in love [4:15–16, NEB]." (See also Romans 12; 1 Corinthians 12—14.) "All of these [ministries]," Paul writes in his first letter to the Corinthians, "must aim at one thing: to build up the church [14:26, NEB]." This drawing together of people into the church, which summons up the language of baptism, eucharist, charisms, and of the Holy Spirit, is important to the servant role. It is when God's people are drawn into the living fellowship of the church by the Holy Spirit that God's word to them, and thence to the world, is known. This is specially the case when God's people gather around the Lord's Table: there, their servant task is reaffirmed and their servanthood is renewed.

Service to fellow members of the church falls directly into the category that the twentieth-century church has termed pastoral care. In Romans 12 and 1 Corinthians 12—13 the references are explicit: Christians should help others in distress cheerfully; contribute to the needs of God's people and practice hospitality; be joyful with those who are joyful; mourn with the mourners; and care as much about one another as they do about themselves. As Christians help one another to bear their "heavy loads," they fulfill the law of Christ (Galatians 6:2).

Servanthood and Suffering

Paul introduces a further image to characterize servants of Christ: through their "new birth," Christians are born into an inheritance that is shared with their Lord. This image points to another trait of servanthood that has its roots in the Old Testament and is refined in the New: the Servant knows suffering, and fellow servants not only should not expect to avoid it, but also are warned that it is endemic to the character of servanthood, serving as a sign and a token of servant status. It is not within the scope of this essay to trace the Old Testament roots of the Suffering Servant image; the New Testament usage, however, cannot be ignored. Paul reminds his readers that suffering is inescapable for fellow slaves with Christ. To be baptized into Christ is to be baptized into suffering. Jesus had warned his disciples of this consequence (John 15:20); they, and their successors, learned the terrible reality at first hand (cf. 1 Corinthians 11:23–33).

This same call and its meaning has been lived out by named and unnamed fellow servants in every age and now comes close to home on the streets and in the parishes not only of Central America and South America, but of the United States as well. The New Testament bears eloquent witness that the very servitude that binds them to Christ as fellow sufferers (2 Timothy 2:11–12; Romans 8:17) liberates Christians from other masters and forms of slavery. So, Paul writes to the Romans:

> You know well enough that if you put yourselves at the disposal of a master, to obey him, you are slaves of the master whom you obey; and this is true whether you serve sin, with death as its result; or obedience, with righteousness as its result. But God be thanked, you, who once were slaves of sin, have yielded whole-hearted obedience to the pattern of teaching to which you were made subject, and, emancipated from sin, have become slaves of righteousness, . . . making for a holy life.
>
> When you were slaves of sin, you were free from the control of righteousness; and what was the gain? Nothing but what now makes you ashamed, for the end of that is death. But now, freed from the commands of sin, and bound to the service of God, your gains are such as make for holiness, and the end is eternal life. For sin pays a wage, and the wage is death, but God gives freely, and his gift is eternal life, in union with Christ Jesus our Lord. (Rom. 6:16–23, NEB; see also Matthew 6:24; Luke 16:13; 1 Corinthians 7:23)

But union with Christ entails readiness to share in his sufferings, and human nature instinctively draws back from the embrace of suffering. Thus, the reality of suffering that is a distinctive feature of the servant role carries with it the temptation to resist that servanthood. It is tempting to look for masters that are less demanding and less threatening to our human desire for physical security and tranquility and that offer speedier and more effortless means to wealth, power, and status. It is even more tempting to avoid the threat of pain, and death itself, on the one hand, or the disaffection and strife that accompanies confrontation with principalities and powers, on the other.

It is a painful reality that it is not only individuals who may become enslaved to "impurity and lawlessness"; the church itself may choose a slavery that compromises its identity and integrity, as it places itself under obligation to other powers. It is then in the impossible position of attempting to be a slave to two masters. In his anguish over the church's perception of its role, Moltmann describes its exodus from a "blinded society" that has psychologically and socially repressed its pain at human suffering, pushing those who suffer to the fringes of society and taking refuge undisturbed in its own activities. For Moltmann, the tragedy of the failure of the church to fulfill its servant role has been the exodus of those of its members who saw it as a church that did not dissociate itself with sufficient determination from enslaving defense mechanisms of society, but rather "enjoyed the religious tolerance of a frigid society, and which, in order to maintain itself in being, has made dishonorable peace and become sterile."[14] A church that has withdrawn from suffering, its own or that of the poor and the oppressed, has, in reality, renounced its servanthood. This also is true for the individual servant.

Perhaps the difficulty with which the Christian servant is confronted is that which Paul identified to the Corinthians— that Christ, and with him his fellow servants, should suffer is scandalous not only to unbelievers, but also to *believers*. It is all very well for theologians to theorize about paradoxes, but believers who practice their faith with integrity may find that a servanthood that liberates them to a life of freedom may be one in which life can only be discovered in dying. Gustav Stahlin addresses this dilemma in his notes on the Greek verb "to scandalize." He indicates that when, in the Gospels, an *en tini* is added to the verb, to indicate the reason for a disciple's falling away, the reference is always to Jesus. Instances are found in Matthew 26:31, 33; 11:6; 13:37; Luke 7:23; and Mark 6:3.

These passages show that *skandalizesthai en auto* can be the opposite of *pisteusai eis auton*. As the Synoptic Jesus often announces His passion, He also predicts a severe crisis for His disciples. Mark 14:27: *pantes skandalisthesesthe*, "you will all give way, fall away (from me)," extended and elucidated in Mt. 26:31: "this night you will all have doubts about me, lose your faith in me."[15]

Two human predispositions operate powerfully to draw us away from the cross, that is, to renounce the servanthood offered by Jesus. First, the social sciences have demonstrated that we intuitively turn away from pain, denying a reality or threat that is too painful to face. The scandal of the cross is that it forces us to decide, consciously and deliberately, whether to take it up. Only in so doing can we choose the freedom that one experiences as a slave of Christ, freedom to know and live life to its fullest, as opposed to becoming enslaved to the passions of self-interest that are associated with preoccupations with affluence, status, or power. Second, we are tempted to reject a servanthood that compels us to take responsibility for our choices and embrace a bondage that is characterized by the *avoidance* of decision-making. Failure to live in accord with Yahweh's purpose constituted evidence that Israel had chosen to serve other gods by default. Israel must learn that not to choose Yahweh is actually to make a choice of the gods of surrounding tribes.

We face the same decisions, although the gods and surrounding tribes may wear different masks. An ordained minister must make the choice of whether to serve the bureaucratic structures of his or her judicatory or the expectations of interest groups; whether, in the words of Moltmann, to fulfill "the public need for cult and sacrifice"; whether, that is, "to serve a part of the whole, rather than the fulness of the Gospel."[16] A business person must decide whether to serve the corporate structures and the values on which they are based, when these involve a confrontation with personal integrity. A spouse may choose the alienation of divorce because that is less painful and less demanding than the struggle to know the partner and be open to him or her. I am not suggesting that any of these social realities is inherently evil or that the decisions arising from them are necessarily immoral or un-ethical. Rather, one may choose to be enslaved to comfort, power, wealth, social status, or ideology in preference to embracing a freedom characterized by fidelity, truth, trust, humility, justice, and compassion. The New Testament sug-gests that the character of the former servitude partakes of the nature of slavery in its profane sense, whereas the latter is characterized by the servant nature embodied by Jesus of Nazareth. And the two are mutually exclusive: what Molt-mann terms "the religion of the cross" bears within it a contradiction, since a servant God is a contradiction in a religion that tacitly acknowledges the gods of comfort, wealth, and power. Answering the summons of the crucified God leads to a servanthood that is very different in nature from that which we are tempted to acknowledge. To accept the former, that is, to make the cross a present reality in our civilization,

> means to put into practice the experience one has received of being liberated from fear for oneself; no longer to adapt oneself to this society, its idols and taboos, its imaginary enemies and fetishes; and in the name of him who was once the victim of religion, society and the state to enter into solidarity with the victims of religion, society and the state at the present day, in the same way as he who was crucified became their brother and their liberator.[17]

The Servant Role of the Church

Moltmann raises in concrete terms the meaning of ser-vanthood for the shaping of the church's servant role in the world. In exploring this corporate aspect of ministry, we dis-cern more of the character of servanthood as lived today. In the upper room, John records Jesus as challenging the twelve:

"I have set you an example; you are to do as I have done for you." This is a command, couched in the form: If you choose to follow me, this will become your way of life.

As noted earlier, one of the implications for the church is that members must be open to serve one another, sensitive to others' needs, eager to support one another, so that the whole body can be built up in love. Important as this nurturing of the body of Christians remains, it is not directed toward some self-serving purpose. Members of the body of Christ are to love their neighbors, expressing in their own individual lives and through the community of the church the love that God has for the world. This mission of the church is one of its fundamental servant tasks. It is a mission popularly under-stood as a witnessing function and may best be expressed in the words of 1 Peter: "You are a chosen race . . . that you may declare the wonderful deeds of him who called you out of darkness into his marvelous light [2:9]." Too often the content of this witnessing function has been viewed narrowly, con-fined to stereotyped methods and formulas of verbal inter-change and challenge to belief in Jesus Christ as Lord. While verbal witness to the redeeming Lord is an obvious channel of ministry, it is not the sole method. Acts of caring ministry in Jesus' name also constitute a ministry of witness. The term "Christian presence" has been coined to express this aspect of ministry. From its earliest use by the worker-priests of France, it has been interpreted to describe a way of life that means much more than merely "being there."

> It tries to describe the adventure of being there in the name of Christ, often anonymously, listening before we speak, hoping that [others] will recognize Jesus for what he is and stay where they are, involved in the fierce fight against all that de-humanizes, ready to act against demonic powers, to identify with the outcast. . . . When we say presence, we say that we have to get into the midst of things even when they frighten us. Once we are there, we may witness fearlessly to Christ if the occasion is given; we may also have to be silent. . . . In one

sense of the word, presence precedes witness. In another sense, the very presence is witness.[18]

This image offers a robust picture of servanthood that incorporates pastoral care as one form that ministry may take, one that stands in its own right alongside the more traditional meanings attached to such words as evangelization, witness, and mission used to describe the church's servant task in the world. Indeed, the concept can be used to argue that the tasks of evangelism and pastoral ministry are inseparably linked, rather than existing as two separate aspects of servanthood. Whether one's exercise of "Christian presence" is in the form of verbal proclamation or is expressed in the form of loving concern that embodies Jesus' compassion for a broken humanity, the intention is to serve by announcing that love. The injunction to love the neighbor is not merely a "law" binding the individual Christian to this service, but applies with the same force to the corporate life of the church as the servant community. Paul calls on the church as the company of God's servants to live in obedience to the "new" law of love, in which our newfound freedom is embodied. The analogy he uses is that of the family. We are reminded that, joined to Christ, we must live not as dependent children, but as adults. Whereas a minor is no better off than a slave ("when we were children, we were slaves to the elemental spirits of the universe"), God's Son is sent to purchase freedom in order that we might attain the status of (adult) sons and daughters (Galatians 4:1–6). The act of salvation confers liberty on former slaves, whose only constraint is the one law by which they are bound—the law of love—which is the new point of departure: "As Paul told the Galatians we have been liberated from the law. But we have not been liberated from it to live any way we choose; we have been liberated to follow a new law, one which is not hanging over us but is rather the very embodiment of our free being: the law of love."[19] Servanthood is now seen to shape all one's relationships, since we are called on to love the neighbor. Paul places this discussion in the context of the Christian's obligations:

> Discharge your obligations to all men; pay tax and toll, reverence and respect, to those to whom they are due. Leave no claim outstanding against you, except that of mutual love. He who loves his neighbour has satisfied every claim of the law. For the commandments, "Thou shalt not commit adultery, thou shalt not kill, thou shalt not steal, thou shalt not covet," and any other commandment there may be, are all summed up in the one rule, "Love your neighbour as yourself." Love cannot wrong a neighbour; therefore the whole law is summed up in love. (Rom. 13:7–10, NEB)

The consequences for the Christian are explicit and concrete. Love of neighbor touches all of one's life. For example, the First Epistle of Peter called on first-century Christians to be subject to every human institution. Leslie Newbigin notes that this form of subjection does not stop at merely obeying civil laws. As Christians, we also participate in the sovereignty to which we have to be subject.[20] Consequently, we bear responsibility for social or societal failures: e.g., for unequal opportunities for education and employment and unequal access to health care. Thus, servanthood obligates the Christian church to play an active role in the secular community and, in particular, to share in Christ's passion for justice for the oppressed. The question is not whether Christians should play an active role in politics, but whether they are prepared to bring their political decisions under the rule of Christ. Christians must allow their servanthood to control all their decisions, not merely limited sections of their decisions, namely, those that concern immediate personal and family ethics. Servanthood is not an attribute that may be confined to selected corners of one's life; it is all-encompassing in its reach and application.

The "liberation theologians" have urged that an uncompromising affirmation of the church's service to the poor and the dispossessed is central to its servanthood, since Jesus came preaching the good news of God to the poor and freedom to the broken victims of human indignities and oppression (Mark 1:14; Luke 4:18–19). It is tragic that in the flare of media publicity devoted to the Vatican's differences with the theologians, the centrality of their message to the church's mission is in danger of being overlooked. This may be due in part to the manner in which they have claimed that God's care for the poor is a *preferential* care. Yet both the Old Testament prophets and the Gospel and epistle writers in the New Testament appear to emphasize just this message. God's servants have a special responsibility not only to act with justice and righteousness, but to speak prophetically to their respective societies in the name of a just and righteous God. Joshua's words ring in our ears also: "Choose this day whom you will serve."

The Servant Community as a Sign

When love for God is expressed both as love for the brotherhood and sisterhood and for the world which is the object of God's love, the church as a company of servants becomes a sign to the world of that community which is God's gift to all creatures. The character of servanthood compels the servant to live as an exemplar of living service, and the community of servants as the first fruits of the society so created. Thus, Stanley Hauerwas calls on each member of the company of servants to be a "sign" of that community into which others may choose to enter. "To be such an interpretative community means that we must be a people transformed by that story." It is not simply a question of just actions and institutions, for example; "rather, we must be a people who are capable of loving the stranger." Such a church is not just "another haven in the storm to protect some from the ravages of modernity, but a people who care so deeply that they refuse to do anything else than speak the truth in love."[21]

42

The community of servants must conform to the character of servanthood embodied by its Lord, if their witness is to have integrity. One of the remarkable passages that bears on the character of this servanthood is the parable of the "Last Judgment." The Matthean author either placed this passage at the close of the account because that was when it was spoken by Jesus—or because, if it is of later origin, the parable was seen to summarize the nature of servant ministry.[22] Caught by surprise when called to enter and possess the kingdom, for they could not imagine on what basis the invitation had been extended, those called righteous were reminded that they had served their Lord throughout their lives. Pressing the Lord further, they are identified as those whose servant ministry is so deeply grounded in their beings that it is of the very essence of their persons. They had ministered not only unostentatiously, but without even making the connection! The force of the message is increased by the identification of the types of service that are listed and the potent manner in which accountability is required: failure to minister, to serve others as a fellow servant of Christ, is cause for judgment.

The expression of love for the neighbor is one form in which the nature of the servant community is manifested. Alexander Miller suggests a second element of the witness that fellow servants are called to make; we are to give human beings bread, not to bear witness that they live by bread alone, but to bear witness that we do not. To Miller's images, Schubert Ogden adds that we not only bear witness that we do not live by bread alone, but also that they do not either.[23] In this sense, servanthood consists in our being signs of that good news, for when we express our care for others, we are witnessing to the belief that they also are given God's love and have the possibility to be free themselves. That is what care means. It is not only that one meets another's immediate needs, but that one has also confronted the other with the possibility that she or he may become a liberated being, liberated from oppressing and soul-destroying slaveries to know the truth that God's love makes one free indeed. If, in that context, the Name can be named (see, for example, Acts 3:6), the appropriateness of doing so will be patent. But "naming the Name" is not indispensable. What is indispensable is what Matthew 25 says is indispensable. The striking note sounded by the parable is that, on Judgment Day, we will apparently not be asked whether we believed in God. We will be asked how we acted in the face of the immediate needs of our neighbors. And we should expect that what holds good on Judgment Day is expected of us here and now.

The servant responsibilities that emerge, given the analysis above, are limited only by the range of needs. They include awareness of the needs of street people and provision for those needs: recognition of the deep alienation that fragments our communities and nation and action to establish paths of reconciliation; identification of those groups that have been oppressed by society and raising one's voice with theirs; openness to those points in civic, state, and national life in which elected representatives go after other gods—power, wealth, ideologies—and fail to fulfill their servant roles. For some servants, it has meant being involved in the Sanctuary movement; for others, speaking out against nuclear proliferation; for still others, standing with unemployed workers and feeling their pain—as much as one person is able to enter into another's pain.

Hauerwas finds that such a community assures him of a second need: it holds its members accountable for the fulfillment of their servant tasks. The notion of accountability, which is inseparable from the character of servanthood, occurs with such frequency in the New Testament that it must either be attributed to Jesus, or the disciples recognized it as one of the fundamental consequences of assuming, with their Master, the form of a slave. It is self-evident that slavery, in the profane sense, was based on the assumption of obedience and accountability. This was no less the assumption of the disciples and their successors. They understood that it is required of stewards that they be found faithful (1 Corinthians 4:2). Further, it is one of the basic lessons enjoined on Christians that every privilege is always "the front end of a responsibility. God only deals with human beings, according to the Bible, by appearing as though a privilege is bestowed, whereas instead God confronts them with new responsibilities; human beings, on the other hand, universally turn every occasion of responsibility into an opportunity for a privilege."[24] The disciples were tempted as we are tempted. They had to learn, as we must learn, that being a fellow servant with Christ is to walk with one who came, not to be served, but to serve. And his fellow slaves are to be held accountable for their servanthood.

When its members fulfill their task of living as signs of the liberated and redeemed community, the fellowship that is thus created and nurtured embodies the character of servanthood to which the Christian community is called. And as I have stated in another context,[25] the church is called to be a sign of the kind of world in which we live and of the kind of world it may become. It is not merely that a Christian or two may, from time to time, speak or act prophetically. It is of the church's *identity* that it *is* prophetic. To that statement it must now be added that it is of the church's identity that it *is* a servant community. The church's prophetic—and pastoral— tasks will only be discerned fully when they are seen as the consequences of the character of its servanthood.

CHAPTER 3

Justice and the Servant Task of Pastoral Ministry

Tom F. Driver

THE TOPIC OF JUSTICE AND PASTORAL MINISTRY IS COM-
plex; and this, I suppose, is the first of many dangers for
anyone daring to address the subject. Before plunging into
the complexities, I want to state my thesis as simply as possible: The pastoral ministry, I hold, has no other object or
obligation except to be in the service of justice. All other ends
that one might envision for the servant task of pastoral ministry, such as to serve God, to serve the gospel of Jesus Christ,
to serve the church, or to serve the other servants of God, are
themselves authentic only insofar as they amount to the service of justice.

In saying this, I aim to take my stand somewhere within the
prophetic tradition, where I also see Jesus to have lived and
died. I am aware that there is also a priestly and a pastoral side
to Christian vocation. My purpose is to show that these, like
the servant role of ministry, are justified only by their devotion to justice.

    Tom F. Driver, Ph.D., is Paul J. Tillich Professor of Theology and Culture,
Union Theological Seminary, New York, New York.

Two Modes of Justice

Simple enough in its initial statement, a justice-oriented interpretation of ministry such as this leads on to numerous complexities. The one in particular that I address now is that justice has more than one mode. We cannot find one simple principle or norm that will everywhere and always define what justice is. The idea of justice shows formal similarity to the idea of God: Both require a *via negativa*. We can more readily discern a case of *in*justice, can know what justice is *not*, than we can define the ideal case of positive justice and know for sure what justice *is*. Our basic ignorance of the ultimate face of justice leads many a person into ethical cynicism, just as many are led to theistic agnosticism by our human inability to define God. The response of faith in both cases is to acknowledge that we confront something transcendent that summons us to a more radical commitment to life.

In this essay I do not stress the *via negativa* as such, but the fact that justice appears in different modalities. In particular, I point to a modality of justice in the society at large and another within the Christian *koinonia*. I argue that these are not two *kinds* of justice, but different modalities of the *same* justice.

There is scarcely a more troublesome theological topic and few more topical than that of the proper understanding of the relation between church and world. In most theological discussion, the church's relation to the world has been subject to an unfortunate dualistic way of thinking. Just as the human person has often been conceived as a kind of centaur—half mind/half body, half soul/half flesh, half reason/half passion— so the church has been viewed as a hybrid institution—half heavenly/half mundane, half theological/half sociological, half out of the world/half in, perhaps in, yet not of. Corresponding to the Chalcedonian formula that described Christ as endowed with two discrete natures in one person, there has been a two-nature concept of the church, which has become, I regret to say, a Sphinx-like Mother, whose nether parts are of an earthly nature, like other social institutions, and whose upper parts are of a heavenly nature, wrapped in mystery and discerned only through eyes of faith. The children of this mother hold dual citizenship—one in earthly society, the other in the City of God.

Like most dualistic expressions, the familiar Christian ones contain enough truth to have given them a long life. But the truth here is so wrongly conceived that it leads to serious, even pernicious, misunderstanding. For example, there is a well-nigh universal tendency, in the presence of a dualism, to regard one side of it as good, the other bad, if not evil. If humans are part soul, part flesh, and if the world is a battleground between Good and Evil, it is difficult to avoid associating the flesh with the devil. Indeed, many dualisms are propounded so as to condemn one part to the realm of evil, or illusion. The evil part good people are asked to repudiate, and thus to split themselves in two. In this way, dualistic religion, a temptation into which monotheisms most readily fall, exacerbates the alienations of human existence and inculcates postures of bad faith.

Liminality

In place of a dualistic concept of church and world, I propose to speak of the church's "liminality." I have taken the idea from the late anthropologist Victor Turner, to whom I am greatly indebted; but I shall explicate the matter in my own fashion, partly so as not to hide my own responsibility under Turner's cloak and partly because an exegesis of his texts is not central to our present purpose.[1]

A *limen*, in the Latin language, is a threshold. In the first decade of this century, Arnold van Gennep analyzed a large class of rituals as "rites of passage,"[2] performed to conduct persons and groups across life's borders, chasms, and thresholds: from infancy over into childhood, for example; from childhood across to adulthood, from private person to public office-holder, from life to death, and so on. He noticed that in such rites there is a stage in which the persons in passage are located ritually in *between* the old and the new. He called this stage "liminal."

Some sixty years later, Victor Turner introduced the idea that all rituals, especially those concerned with supernatural powers, can be characterized by their liminality, which we may think of as their "in between-ness," their separation from ordinary time, ordinary space, and, most important, ordinary behavior. The obligations and customs of the daily world were spoken of by Turner, in the jargon of anthropology, as "social structure." He meant by that term another and very peculiar modality of structure, a structure contrived to point, so to speak, toward no structure at all. The aim he detected in religious ritual is to pass from a familiar social rank, and experiences of alienation, into an alternate structure, there to enter on a time and space in which the human estrangements built into the dominant social structure are cast aside. This new condition, beyond alienation, beyond separation, beyond mediation, Turner called "communitas." We may think of it as a state of communal blessedness.

The most highly rational forms of Christianity, whether liberal or fundamentalist, appear to have forgotten what Turner calls "communitas." It would be well for them to recover this and link it with the pursuit of justice. The vocation of the Christian ecclesia, according to much of the theological tradition, is to exist as a people who have been called forth from one world to exist in preparation for another. The church bears witness to a kingdom, realm, or commonwealth that we have been told to expect as a new creation from God and of which we have presentiment in the sacramental, that is to say, the communitarian, life of the church. Christians, then, to the extent that they are graced with faith, to the extent that they are Christian not solely from a sociological point of view, but also from a religious or gospel-praxis point of view, are between worlds. They are liminal.

Unlike a moat or a wall, a threshold is meant to be crossed. It not only divides, but also unites. One should cross a threshold not by accident or necessity, but with voluntary intention. A threshold of ritual liminality should be crossed repeatedly in both directions. To this crossing of the threshold I shall return after speaking of the terrain on both its sides.

Structural Mode

On one side of the liminal divider lies what Turner calls social structure. The biblical term for it is "world." It is the domain of institutions, of social hierarchy, and of work. It is, most of the time, exceedingly powerful, determining the objective conditions under which people live. It is the domain of justice and injustice, as these are usually understood. Within the social structure, justice must be understood in a social structural modality. In this mode, justice means actions and policies that are regulated by wisdom, reason, and law. Law is supposed to protect persons within the social structure from abuses of power. At the same time, however, any society's laws grant privilege to some members and deny it to others. As Marx put it, laws reflect the ideology and the self-interest of the ruling class. They determine, even within democracies, various grades within the social structure, ranking people according to some principle of order. In our society this order is mostly based on money, although race and gender also come into it. In some societies the ranking order is based on lineage, on religion, on elitist training, and so on.

Before laws were codified, societies expected justice to emanate from the wisdom of good rulers. Even societies governed "by law and not by men" still depend on the wisdom of just judges to interpret the law and of legislators to enact it. The wisdom of judges and rulers, like the justness of laws, is measured by reason. Without the critique of reason, arbitrariness and unfairness find their way into the judgments of even the kindest of rulers and into the framing of laws. Within the domain of social structure, wisdom, reason, and law are the three great pillars of justice, and in this modality, justice itself, like the society of which it is a part, is envisioned as a structure.

It is crucial, when thinking of the social structural mode of justice, to remember that it is designed to cope with conflict. The problem of social justice is not just a problem of bringing actions under the judgment of reason: it is the problem of finding structures to minimize the resolve to compete among antagonistic groups. In its social modality, justice is a structure of defense erected against omnipresent conflict and its resultant injustices. To view justice as a defensive structure is insufficient in the long run, but it is quite necessary as far as it goes. Without any doubt, reason, law, and wisdom are needed to defend the weaker members of society from the stronger, the poor from the rich, the small from the great, the minority from the majority, the unskilled worker from the ruthless labor market, an oppressed racial, cultural, or sexual group from those who dominate. In its social modality, justice is whatever structure—ideational, legal, institutional, political, or even military—that protects the disadvantaged against those who would exploit them. Needless to say, such structures seldom work as well as they are supposed to do.

Identifying with Victims

Before turning to the other side of the threshold, let me call attention to one of the foremost tasks of pastoral ministry with regard to social justice. It is to pay attention. I mean specifically to pay attention to the cries of those whom the social structure of justice has not adequately protected and whose suffering and pain are therefore inflicted by the social structure itself. I have said that the pastoral minister is the servant

51

of justice and nothing else. I now add that this servanthood has its foundation in an ability to identify with the victims of injustice. American rhetoric speaks often of compassion, but I prefer the word identification because it is more radical and because it is closer to Christian incarnational theology, in which God not only looks with compassion on the human race, but also identifies with it even to the point of death.

Being a martyr and playing Jesus are not what I wish to encourage. Only in rare circumstances should we say that the pastoral servant is called to die. I encourage, however, identification with the poor and, out of such identification, the raising of one's voice in solidarity with society's victims. A good servant of justice will teach others to listen for those cries and will build a company of human beings who are willing to speak and act on behalf of those who need help from heaven because the social structure is unjust to them. Their number increases rapidly today in our own society and almost everywhere else in the world. Structures of social justice are breaking down because of the greed and fear of empires that are both nationalistic and corporate. But this is happening also, I fear, because many religious leaders, many pastors, and many laity view themselves as having some other servanthood than that of justice. In that circumstance, wisdom, reason, and law prove inadequate to the human situation, since they do not reach to the religious dimension of justice. Class warfare is unleashed, and the social structures are threatened by anarchy. In most cases the victims are blamed for this.

Today, under the deliberately deceptive gloss of synthetic apple pie Americanism, this nation's structures of social justice are being ravaged. Millions of unemployed, under-nourished, and culturally deprived Americans are paying dearly. The economic security of the middle class is also threatened. Our children probably will see economic, perhaps also political, chaos—not because of external pressures on the United States, but because there are within our land an insufficient number of servants of justice. This is true despite the fact that we are a great churchgoing society. There are simply not enough servants of justice in our religious communities. Now let us turn to the other side of the threshold.

The Communitarian Mode

Religious communities are alternative structures. Their heart lies in their ritual life, which Turner spoke of as anti-structural. Protestants, by and large, do not much like to speak of ritual, but we mean the same if we refer to services of worship, to liturgy, to revival meetings, to preaching services, to hymn sings, to prayer meetings, or to any other similar activity. All are structures of performance created by the church, yielding experiences that are antithetical to those provided by the social structure. The core quality of these experiences, which may be found in rituals of virtually all religions, Victor Turner named *communitas*. He meant not only the ideal, but also the experience, however momentary, of relating to other human beings who are *outside* the formalities, the mediations, and the hierarchical rankings of the social structure. *Communitas* is communal and communitarian existence. Social structure sets limits to this and often destroys it. Ritual gatherings, especially in religious forms, provide a time and a space for its instantiation. In the language of Christian tradition, *communitas* is called *koinonia*, or fellowship, or the communion of saints, or the blessed company of the believers. It is marked by grace, and its prime symbol is the eucharistic table.

It is tempting to imagine that when we cross the threshold from the harsh world of social structure into the alternative world of worship and sacrament, we have crossed into a realm of blessedness in which the question of justice is left behind, but this is not so. By crossing the threshold we pass into an anti-structure in which justice is still justice, although it appears in another modality. I shall call this mode *communitarian*. In its communitarian mode, justice is envisioned in

53

its positive rather than its defensive aspect. In this mode, justice is seen to be not only protective, but also joyful. It is revealed to be not merely the absence of injustice, but the abundance of life in harmony.

I stated earlier that justice, being transcendent, cannot be seen directly, but only by *via negativa*. That is true of justice in its social modality, but in its communitarian mode, justice reveals glimpses of itself, just as, in the religious life of worship and praise, God is revealed in images and stories that pass beyond the *via negativa* required by the structures of reasons. The anti-structures of religious ritual are highly imaginative, conjuring visions of the truth we worship. These visions do not properly belong in the public social structure on the secular side of the threshold: The baby Jesus in his crèche on the town square and the prayer introduced into the school are very likely to occasion injustice. The deep social justice reasons for separating church and state are not understood by Ronald Reagan in this country nor by the Ayatollah Khomeini in his. They confuse and conflate the different modalities of justice. On the anti-structural side, however, positive images of God and of justice are powerful and lifegiving. They are the instrumentalities through which God and people communicate and in which we discover that justice is not only a matter of doing the best you can with a cruel world, but it is also holy. It is the pearl of great price. It is full of grace and peace.

Love Belongs to Justice

What I am calling the communitarian mode of justice is frequently spoken of as love. Love is certainly a vital component of *communitas*. But we pay a high price for denying to communal love the name of justice. For one thing, we lose sight of the fact that justice has a communitarian mode and an angelic face as well as a structural mode and a stern face. For another, our separation of love from justice leads to the sentimentalizing of love, so that love becomes all tender feeling and is often privatized, losing its connection with the life of groups. It is better to see that love is an ingredient of justice in its communitarian mode and that it stands, so to speak, in the shadow, lending its influence to every act of justice in the structural mode as well. Love is not something different from justice, but something within justice that is longing to show itself.

Perhaps an analogy will be useful. We can think of music in two ways. We can regard it as the notes on a page and the laws of composition, as everything one might study in a course on musicology. That would, I suppose, be music in its structural mode. Whether such knowledge be transmitted by formal schooling or by oral tradition, no society can have a tradition of music without it. But there is something else that we call music that cannot be learned in musicology. It is the quality, the beat, the lyric impulse, the "soul," if you please, that makes music musical. The soul of music is not something other than music. It is the music of music. It is the reason there is music in heaven and none in hell, even if they may have an orchestra there.

Using such an analogy, we can say that there is justice in heaven. We may, if we like, say that love is the soul of justice, but we dare not say that love is something other than justice. When we say, as we do, that God is love, we should realize that we are also saying that God is justice. Pastoral ministers are called to be the servants of God whose love is made visible in justice and whose gospel is practiced through devotion to justice. Let us think once again of the threshold.

Crossing and Re-crossing the Threshold

Church and world do not stand in a complementary relation one to another, but in a dialectical relation. Perhaps I had better say that when their relation becomes complementary rather than dialectical, the justice of God is betrayed. The purpose of the Christian church, with its worship of God and its rejoicing in the Holy Spirit, is not to provide a vacation from the winter of worldly care. It is not to provide a shelter in the wilderness nor a way station for souls who are getting saved and passing on toward God's heaven in some place remote from the socially structured world. Communitarian justice is not a mere antidote or recompense for all the labor we have to devote to structural justice. No, the purpose of the Christian anti-structures is to provide witness, experience, and envisionment to be carried back across the threshold as news, resource, and motivation for the transformation of the social world. The existence of the communitarian mode of justice acts as a rebuke to social structure. It keeps it off balance. It releases the *communitas* that the social structure keeps clamped down, thereby exposing the contradiction that lies at the heart of social structure, turning that contradiction into a motor force for the transformation of society in historical process.

Conversely, the structural mode of justice is often needed to discipline religious anti-structures when they have sentimentalized themselves, or turned their backs on the struggles within society, or betrayed the communitarian mode of justice by turning the church family into something hierarchical or bureaucratic or autocratic. When this happens, God comes to despise our feast days, withdrawing the Spirit from us and using the structural modalities of the world like a rod of chastisement against us, forcing the church to treat its own members with at least that minimal measure of justice that the surrounding society has institutionalized. We get, then, the ugly but, unfortunately, necessary spectacle of a pastor suing the bishop in a court of law because the disciplinary procedures inside the church have not met the society's minimal standards of due process.

The service of God calls us to make regular and frequent moves across the threshold dividing the structures of society from the anti-structures of religious worship and praise. If the threshold has been made too high, and if crossing it in both directions is not sufficiently intentional, the religious community will find itself not liminal, but marginal. Instead of being in a dialectically critical and creative passage *between* the secular and the sacred, it will be relegated to an irrelevant existence at the margin of society, where it either makes no forays into public life or else does so with no discernible influence that has been generated by this experience of the justice of God in the communitarian mode. The former is the fate of many sect groups; the latter is the sad plight of religion domesticated to the social status quo.

Words of Admonition

Having said all this, I offer two words of admonition to the churches. The first is that in America, if not also elsewhere, most Christian worship, having lost its fervor, is of little use to the service of justice. Partly the churches' services of worship have remained too patriarchal, so that the social structural sin of male dominance prevails also in the house of God, where it mixes with racism and classism to drive out that *communitas* with which the Spirit of God would like to fill the church. The churches give lip service to equality, but most do not practice it even within the region that is open to them, namely, the rituals on the anti-structural side of the threshold.

For this reason, and also because of the prevailing rationalism of our culture, the churches frequently fail to think of justice in anything other than structural mode. If we do any justice at all, it is usually to preach of it and organize for it and organize for it almost entirely in the same terms as are used in the political and legal spheres. We do not much employ, even within the church itself, the lyric and ecstatic visions of justice that we ought to be learning in our experiences of justice in the communitarian mode. Having lost ecstasy, we have lost touch with the ultimate spirit of justice. It is little wonder that some people accuse the churches of selling out to secularity. I am aware that such an accusation is often motivated by a desire for the churches not to agitate for civil rights, disarmament, economic reform, and other progressive causes. But the fact is that many pastoral servants of justice fail to contribute anything distinctive to the public debates, for they fail to give witness to the divine gift of justice that we ought to have experienced in eucharist. We debate when we should say, like Martin Luther King, "I have been to the mountain!"

The second admonition is a reminder of the actual situation of justice as it is practiced within church institutions. I speak now of the governance structures, not of the anti-structures of worship about which I was speaking a moment ago, although the two topics are related. The record is not good. The structures in our churches are bureaucratic, patriarchal, and hierarchical in the extreme. When the United Methodist Church, the denomination of which I am a member, moved in 1984 to forbid to homosexual persons permission to be ordained or to receive a pastoral appointment, justice was neither the end in view nor the manner chosen to reach it. No homosexual minister whom I know—and that includes a fair number—was so much as consulted on the question. Not much theological opinion was sought. If ethicists were consulted, their opinions were not widely published. The church was in stampede to rid itself of a potential embarrassment, for which injustice, including hypocrisy, looked like a small price to pay. I ask: Where has the communitarian mode of justice been all these years in the Methodist Church that so many of its pastoral-ministerial servants of justice could suddenly find themselves namelessly anathematized? Although the legislative decision itself was sudden, the failure of communitarian justice that led up to it was not. The decision revealed that we are a church that does not know, and does not want to know, even its own members, let alone the stranger in the public square.[3]

The Roman Catholic Church is in a similar position regarding all issues surrounding sexuality: birth control, abortion, celibacy, homosexuality, and the status of women. In these matters, and some others, there is no wish of the hierarchy to go looking for what is just, only to impose, as if by the Divine Right of Bishops, some decisions made long ago—and for that matter, not made at the beginning of the church, but later, when Christianity became ascetic and misogynistic.

The churches' attitudes toward poverty are only slightly better than their attitudes toward sex. In the United States there is almost no church forum in which the poor are listened to as if their right to be heard is equal to that of the wealthy. In church councils, as elsewhere, money talks. And this puts most pastoral ministers in an awkward position regarding the service of justice: What protection have they if they champion the cause of the poor and spend time among them? At present, it is generally presumed, by many laity as well as by denominational officials, that the pastoral minister's first task is to serve the church. This assumption puts the churches on the road to irrelevance. Surely Jesus' injunction to seek first the "kingdom of God" means that the first task of Christian ministry is to serve justice, in both its modes.

Revolutionary Expectation

The communitarian mode of justice should prevent Christians from assuming that social structures are always to be preserved. The justice of God is not confined to, and certainly not identical with, the structures of any given society. All stand under judgment of communitarian justice. This means that sometimes Christian solidarity with the victims of the social structure must lead to solidarity with revolution. A church that does not keep alive in its people the possibility of supporting revolution is in fact captive to the social structure. In the last analysis it has no word of liberation, for it will have assumed that all earthly powers, no matter how unjust, are in the service of God. This easily turns into the idea that the government under which one lives is actually doing the will of God, and to suppose this is to forget justice in its communitarian mode. The tragedy of the United States today is that most Americans cannot identify with any of the revolutions that are going on—not those in Central America, not the one shaping up in South Africa, not those in the Middle East, scarcely even the resistance movements in Afghanistan and Poland. North Americans cannot well make such identification because they have ceased to imagine that they might ever again need a revolution themselves.

The servant task of pastoral ministry is to make and encourage identification with those whom the social structures victimize. It is to move with one's fellow Christians very intentionally and very frequently in both directions across the threshold between structural modes of justice and the communitarian modes of justice that are afforded by the worship of God. It is to keep ever alive in oneself and in others the knowledge that no known structures of justice and no known ritual anti-structures devoted to *communitas* are yet perfect. A faithful servant of the gospel is prepared to seek their replacement whenever the way is open to the increase of justice in the world.[4]

CHAPTER 4

The Servant Church

James H. Cone

MUCH HAS BEEN WRITTEN ABOUT THE CHURCHES DURING the course of their historical development. Ernst Troeltsch, H. Richard Niebuhr, and Peter Paris[1] have written about the social origin and teaching of the Christian churches, and others, like Williston Walker, Carter G. Woodson, E. Franklin Frazier, and Sydney Alstrom,[2] have concentrated on their institutional history. Systematic and historical theologians, like Karl Barth, Cyril Richardson, Jürgen Moltmann, and Hans Küng,[3] with special interest in their transcendent origin, have focused their attention on the doctrinc of the church. But whether one speaks of the social origin and teaching of the Christian churches, their institutional history, or their theological essence, none of these foci should be isolated from the others because each is important for the formulation of a meaningful, contemporary definition of the church.

Every generation of Christians should ask: What is it that constitutes our identity, and thus empowers us to live it out in

James H. Cone, Ph.D., is Charles A. Briggs Professor of Systematic Theology, Union Theological Seminary, New York, New York.

the world? To answer this question we must focus on the institutional and ethical activity that validates our ecclesiological confessions. If we separate the doctrine of the church from its historical embodiment in our congregational life, we will also ignore the social and political significance of our creedal formulations. Therefore, whatever else we may advance as our definition of the church, we should never separate the doctrine of the church from empirical, local congregations. Although a theological doctrine of the church attempts to point to "more" than what can be empirically observed in local congregations, this "theological more," involved in an ecclesial self-definition, is itself obscured and distorted when it is separated from particular congregations and their behavior in the world. This means that the "more" that may be disclosed in a theology of the church can only be found through a critical analysis of the sociology of the churches.

What, then, is the relationship between *the* church and local congregations, between a theology of the church and a sociology of the churches? Unfortunately, theologians have tended to give an inordinate amount of attention to the doctrine of the church, an ecclesiological perspective that seems to exist nowhere in society except in their minds and textbooks. This clever ecclesiological sophistry enables pastors and other church officials to justify existing church institutions without seriously inquiring about their historical faithfulness to the gospel message that they claim as the foundation of the church's identity. By focusing their attention on a doctrinal understanding of the church that has little sociological relevance, theologians can easily ignore obvious historical contradictions and shortcomings of empirical churches. This abstract theological maneuver in their analyses of the church's identity makes it possible for theologians to speak of the church as the "body of Christ" without saying a word about its relation to broken human bodies in society.

By focusing on the sociology of the churches and on their privileged political status in this society, churchpeople may be able to see themselves as others see them, and thus partly guard against innocuous theological speech. Too often churches have been guilty of covering up their own sins behind sophisticated theological jargon. While saying that we are concerned about the poor, we do not analyze and fight against the socioeconomic structures that are responsible for their poverty. To be sure, many congregations have food programs, jail and hospital ministries, and other special projects designed to "help" the needy and the unfortunate. But such projects are not designed to challenge the capitalist system that creates human misery. Churches are often incapable of attacking the root cause of oppression because they are benefactors of the sociopolitical system that is responsible for it. It is because churches are so much a reflection of the values of the society in which they exist that they also have a serious credibility problem among people who regard their poverty and imprisonment as a by-product of an unjust social order. A poem circulated at a poor people's rally in Albuquerque, New Mexico, entitled "Listen, Christians," describes a perspective of the church that churchpeople do not like to hear.

> I was hungry
> and you formed a humanities club
> and you discussed my hunger.
> Thank you.
>
> I was imprisoned
> and you crept off quietly
> to your chapel in the cellar
> and prayed for my release.
>
> I was naked
> and in your mind
> you debated the morality of
>   my appearance.

I was sick
and you knelt and thanked God
    for your health.

I was homeless
and you preached to me
of the spiritual shelter of
    the love of God.

I was lonely
and you left me alone
to pray for me.
You seem so holy;
so close to God.
But I'm still very hungry
and lonely
and cold.

So where have your prayers
    gone?
What have they done?
What does it profit a man
to page through his book of prayers
when the rest of the world
is crying for his help?

This poem exposes the hypocrisy of the churches and forces one to ask whether any ecclesial confession is ever valid apart from a concrete, practical activity that validates it. How can one speak about the church as the body of the crucified Jesus of Nazareth when churchpeople are so healthy and well fed and have no broken bones? Can we really claim that established churches are the people of God when their actions in society blatantly contradict the one who makes that identity possible?

My intention is not to ridicule and poke fun at the churches. I am a member of the church, and I have been one of its ministers since I was sixteen years old, with pastorates in Little Rock, Arkansas, at San Hill, Spring Hill, and Allen Chapel A.M.E. churches. Because of my love and concern for the church I, as one of its theologians, must subject it to severe criticism when it fails to be in society what it confesses to be in worship. Because our so-called theological jargon about the church has become so insensitive to human pain and suffering, and thus a distortion of an authentic Christian calling, it would be helpful if we could return to the concrete social reality of our existence, so that we may be permitted to move to a deeper theological level. We cannot experience the deeper level of our theological identity until we have immersed ourselves in the social matrix in which our identity must be actualized. For this reason a social analysis of the churches must precede a doctrine of the church. We should never allow a theological interpretation of the church's transcendent origin to obscure the empirical behavior of churches that deny what churchpeople affirm in their ecclesiological confessions. The presence of the transcendent element in the church's identity should always point to a concrete, recognizable human community that attempts to embody in history what is being said in the theological framework of our ecclesiology. If what we say in our theological definition of the church is not observable in our congregational life, then why should anyone believe what we say? If what we say about the church as the body of Christ, the people of God, and the new covenant fails to create a theological challenge that also informs and directs a congregation's social and political behavior, then how do we know that what we say is not a figment of our theological imagination? We can talk about the one, holy, apostolic, and catholic church from now to the end of time. But unless our words and phrases point to some recognizable referent in actual congregations, then we have a docetic, invisible church. To help protect ourselves against this error, we pastors, theologians, and churchpeople must become aware that a critical sociological component is needed in every theological definition of the church.

While a sociology of the churches should serve as the starting point for an analysis of the theology of the church, it nonetheless is important to point out that theology and sociology in the context of the church and the churches are not identical. When I speak of a sociology of the churches, I have in mind that which can be empirically observed by the tools of critical research. But is not the Christian church more than what can be observed through a scientific examination of denominational churches? At least many theologians, preachers, and church members think so. These persons believe that the church has a divine origin from which it derives its essential identity. It is in the context of faith that theologians affirm that we cannot allow the meaning of the church to be exclusively derived from the imperfections of the churches.

Despite what some persons might think, I still believe in the transcendent foundation of the church. I only wish to emphasize that we churchpeople, especially theologians and pastors, have been too carried away by that theological option and, as a result, have distorted its true meaning. The transcendent origin of the church has been used as a camouflage to cover up the gross shortcomings of so-called Christian churches. If we want honestly to face up to who we really are and who we really represent, then we must not evade the tough, uncomfortable questions that expose the churches for what they are. For example, does not the theological claim that the church has its origin in God conflict sharply with a social analysis of the churches that shows that the activities of denominations and local congregations are no different from those of other social institutions? As churchpeople, is it not claiming much too much to say that what we represent is of God, when our actions clearly originate from the values of a racist, classist, and sexist society?

Furthermore, even if it is agreed that the church has its origin beyond the context of this world, it is still necessary to face honestly the question: What is the relation between the theology of the church and a sociology of the churches? The way out of this dilemma is not a bold theological affirmation that "the Christian church is the church of Jesus Christ." Rather, the acid test of any ecclesiological statement is found in whether it has taken into sufficient account the sociological world in which liturgical confessions are made. The transcendent can be encountered only in the particularity of a human situation. Whatever else the transcendent may mean, it is always relevant to and for human beings. This is the significance of the incarnation, God becoming human in Jesus. It is the incarnation that necessitates our sociological starting point. To be sure, the sociological without the theological reduces the church to a social club of like-minded people. But the theological without a critical sociological component makes the church a non-historical, spiritual community whose existence has no effect on our social and political environment. My concern is to examine the theological understanding of the church in the context of its sociopolitical existence in the world.

The Interrelationship of the Church, Jesus Christ, and the Poor

The Christian church is that community of people called into being by the life, death, and resurrection of Jesus. The beginning and the end of the church's identity is found in Jesus Christ and nowhere else. He is the one who is the subject of the church's preaching and the one who embodies in his person the meaning of its mission in the world. To ask, "What is the church?" is also to ask, "Who is Jesus?" for without Jesus the church has no identity. That was why Paul referred to the church as the body of Christ and why many theologians, past and present, would adhere to the claim that every ecclesiological statement is, at the same time, a christological statement.

The differences among the churches, therefore, have not focused at the point of whether Christ is to be regarded as the head of the church. All churches that bear the name Christian would adhere to the confession that "Jesus Christ is Lord." Rather, the differences among the churches that prevent their unity arise from the theological and sociological implications of that christological confession. When the churches begin to spell out the structural meanings of Jesus' lordship for congregational life and for participation in society, they often find themselves in sharp disagreement. What does it mean to declare that Jesus is the head of the church whose sovereignty extends to the whole world? Not all churches answer that question the same way.

Another factor worth noting has been the churches' inordinate preoccupation with the *theological* side of their identity, as if their transcendent origin legitimated their privilege in society and bestowed on their ministry a similar privilege in judgment regarding how the society should be politically, socially, and economically arranged. From the early church to the present there have been intense debates regarding the precise meaning of the *ekklesia*. But the discussions have focused primarily on the church's specifically *divine* origin in order to defend its privilege against "heretics," rather than in defense of the poor, which the divine origin entails. This distorted emphasis on the theological, almost to the exclusion of the need to make political solidarity with the poor and against their oppressors, has often blinded churches to their responsibility to implement in society what they sometimes confess in worship.

In his debate with the Donatists, Augustine, for example, defined the church in terms of the four marks of unity, holiness, catholicity, and apostolicity, with an emphasis also on its visible and invisible nature. John Calvin and his supporters of the magisterial Reformation added two marks: "the Word of God purely preached and heard and the sacraments administered according to Christ's institution."[4] The Radical Reformation also added several marks, one of which was obedience to the "Cross of Christ which is borne for the sake of his testimony and Word."[5] Menno Simons, a representative of this Radical tradition, rejected the inordinate emphasis on the invisibility of the church. According to him, "as long as the transgressors and willful despisers of the holy Word are unknown to the church she is innocent, but when they are known and then not excluded after proper admonition, but allowed to remain in the fellowship . . . then . . . she ceases to be the church of Christ."[6] Simons' concern, along with other Anabaptists, was the *restitution* of the church along the lines of its apostolic pattern. That was why *discipline* became one of the essential marks of the church. Unlike Augustine and Calvin, who contended that the true church was invisible, and thus known only to God by virtue of divine election, the Anabaptists insisted that the church of Christ is an "assembly of the pious." Although Calvin could say that "the pure ministry of the Word and pure mode of celebrating the sacraments" are sufficient for the church's identity, "even if it otherwise swarms with many faults,"[7] Menno Simons contended that "we know for sure where . . . there is no pious Christian life, no brotherly love, and no orthodox confession, there no Christian church is."[8]

Although sharp differences exist between Augustine and Calvin, on the one hand, and Menno Simons and his Anabaptist supporters, on the other, there is a striking similarity among them from the perspective of their concentrated preoccupation with the theological or the transcendental origin of the church. This transcendent focus has often prevented churchpeople from seeing the correct relationship between theology and politics, the preaching of the gospel to the poor and its implementation in society. During the sixteenth century the Anabaptists appeared to have come closest to recognizing the cross of Jesus as essential for the church's life of suffering. For they insisted that "the True Church was a suffering church whose changing patterns were ever cast in the shadow of the Man Upon the Cross."[9] But, unfortunately, they tended to become too sectarian by withdrawing from social and political responsibility and thereby reinforcing the idea that the church is a specifically spiritual institution.

It was Karl Marx, and later the sociologists of knowledge,

who pointed out that the churches' emphasis on the specifically theological was, in fact, a camouflage for their support of the existing social order. The churches are not really non-political, even though they often have said that "the church should stay out of politics." As the active participation of the Moral Majority in electoral politics has demonstrated, this dictum holds true for many white conservative churchpeople only as long as the existing social order is not disturbed. If a threat to the "law and order" of the system exists, the churches will take the lead in providing a sacred justification for all so-called good people to take up arms against the forces of evil.

It was because the churches and their leaders provided a theological justification for an unjust social order that Marx defined religion as the opiate of the people. Whether Marx was correct in his judgment is still a much debated issue, with churchpeople insisting that they represent more than a "sacred canopy"[10] of their social environment. Regardless of what churchpeople claim about themselves in their worship and intellectual lives, it seems that the burden of proof is on them to validate their claims of transcendence. And this validation must involve more than intellectual or pietistic appeals to God. Churchpeople must be able to point to something in their congregational life that is not simply a religious legitimation of the values of the social order in which they live.

The need for the church to act against itself in order to be its true self has been pointed out by both theologians and social ethicists. For example, Langdon Gilkey has said: "Since the church is *in* secular culture, . . . the life of the congregation cannot in any sense express transcendence of the culture around it unless it is willing to challenge the injustice . . . of the wider community in which it lives."[11] With a firmer grasp of the tools of social analysis, James Gustafson is even more insightful in his comments about the churches. Gustafson is concerned about the sharp distinction that is made between the public life and the private life and the limitation of the church to the latter. But even in the private sphere, the church's "role has become supportive, therapeutic, pastoral and even idolatrous, for it functions to give religious sanctions to a culturally defined pattern of life that is itself not sufficiently subjected to theological and moral criticism."[12] One test of the authenticity of the church's claim to transcendence is its capacity to represent in its congregation a "socially heterogeneous" people. If it is not possible for blacks and whites to worship and practice the Christian faith in the world as *one* community because of radically different cultural mores, can we not conclude that their respective racial groupings are due to each people's values and not to the work of God's Spirit? Jesus Christ breaks down the barriers that separate people (Galatians 3:21).

> The physical presence of heterogeneity makes it more difficult for a congregation to confuse a particular social mode of life with the religiously acceptable and divinely ordained one. . . . Moral concerns brought under the conditions of social and cultural diversity could not be simply the projection of the ideology of a particular interest group on the screen of divine approval.[13]

It is unfortunate that Gilkey's and Gustafson's points about transcendence have not been forcefully advanced so as to shake up the social and political complacency of white churches. Established white churches have almost always focused on the specifically theological understanding of their identity, which also has usually led to a conservative approach to politics, especially in race relations. One can examine the attitude of white churches toward African slavery, and with few exceptions, their views functioned as a religious legitimation of their social and political interests. Many whites openly justified slavery as ordained of God, quoting Paul's "slaves be obedient to your master" as the evidence. Others, being a little more sophisticated, ignored the issue altogether, as if one's attitude toward human servitude had nothing to do with

71

the gospel of Jesus. Another group, while admitting that slavery was immoral and should be abolished, advocated a gradual, nonconflictual approach to its abolition. It is revealing that similar attitudes were found among white churchpeople regarding lynching, school integration, civil rights, black power, and poverty. With regard to justice and peace for persons who are not of European descent, the great majority of white churchpeople (conservative and liberal, right and left, theologians, pastors and laypeople) seem to reflect in their religion the values of the existing racist and capitalist socioeconomic order.

Gustafson explains the support of white clergy and theologians of the existing social order in this way.

> Like all beings, the clergy and the theologians are more comfortable if they can blame what is wrong on forces outside themselves. . . . Clergy and theologians can find as good excuses as any man to deny any responsibility for what is happening to the community and mission with whose leadership they are charged. If there is any sense of repentance, it is all too often, like a general confession of sin, vague and undifferentiated. It leads to a certainty of guilt for the ills of the Church but does not move in the direction of overcoming those ills.[14]

Whatever else the Christian faith may mean, it is never a reflection of the values of the dominant culture. That was why God elected Hebrew slaves and not Egyptian slave masters as the covenant people. That was also why the prophets defined God's justice as punishment of the oppressor and liberation of the poor. In a similar vein but at a much deeper level, the birth, life, teachings, death, and resurrection of Jesus means that God turns the world's value system upside down. No one expressed this point any clearer than the apostle Paul:

> It was to shame the wise that God chose what is foolish by human reckoning, and to shame what is strong that he chose what is weak by human reckoning; those whom the world

72

thinks common and contemptible are the ones that God has chosen—those who are nothing at all to show up those who are everything. (1 Cor. 1:27–28, JB)

If the community of white churches expect to be taken seriously about their claim to be of God, then they must begin to act against the social order and ecclesiastical structures that do not affirm the humanity of people of color.

It is important to note the contrast between black churches and white churches in the United States during slavery and the civil rights movement of the 1950s and 1960s. For example, when white preachers and missionaries introduced their version of Christianity to African slaves, many slaves rejected it by contending that God willed their freedom and not their servitude. Separate and independent black congregations began to develop among slaves and free Africans in the North and the South because black people did not believe that a segregated congregational life in which they were treated as second-class Christians was reconcilable with their view of the lordship of Jesus over the church. If Jesus Christ is the Lord of the church and the world, as white confessions claimed, then church institutions that claim the Christian identity must reflect their commitment to him in the congregational life of the church as well as in its political and social involvement in society. When northern black Methodists and Baptists formed independent church institutions in Philadelphia, New York, and Baltimore, and when southern blacks created a secret, "invisible institution" in Alabama, Georgia, Arkansas, and Mississippi, their actions in both contexts suggested that some black people recognized the connection between theology and politics, between the confession of faith in church worship and the political commitment that validated it in society. Expressing her reaction to the sermons of white preachers, Hanna Austin, an ex-slave from Georgia, said: "We seldom heard a true religious sermon: but we were constantly preached the doctrine of obedience to masters and mis-

73

tresses."[15] One white preacher interpreted Christian obedience to black slaves in this way: "The Lord says . . . if you are good to your masters and mistresses, He has got a kitchen in heaven and you will all go there by and by."[16]

But African slaves knew that God had more than a kitchen waiting for them, and their experience of this "eschatological more" in Jesus Christ necessitated the formation of a congregational life so that their christological encounter could be liturgically celebrated. Minnie Ann Smith, an ex-slave, reflected on her presence in the church as an "invisible," secret, but historical institution: "We slips off and have prayer but daren't 'low the white folks to know it and sometimes we hums 'ligious songs low like when we's working. It was our way of prayin' to be free, but the white folks didn't know it."[17] In this quotation a different perspective on the invisible church is suggested. It is an invisibility grounded not (as with Augustine and Calvin) in divine election, but in a religious conviction about the lordship of Christ that had to be lived out in history and in the midst of an extreme situation of political oppression.

It is unfortunate that many black churches of today have strayed from their liberating heritage. Instead of deepening their commitment to the poor in their community and in the Third World, many, more often than not, have adopted the same attitude toward the poor as the white churches from which they separated. Too many black churches are more concerned about buying and building new church structures than they are about feeding, clothing, and housing the poor. Too many pastors are more concerned about how to manipulate people for an increase in salary than they are about liberating the oppressed from sociopolitical bondage. If black churches do not repent by reclaiming their liberating heritage for the empowerment of the poor today, their Christian identity will be no more authentic than the white churches that segregated them.

It is revealing that the modern search for unity among the churches focused on *confessional* unity, and neither white nor black churches of the United States objected to that limited focus. When the World Council of Churches (WCC) was organized at Amsterdam in 1948, its unity was based on the confession of "Jesus Christ as God and Savior." There was no reference to the political and social significance of this confession. But the subsequent numerical increase of Asians, Africans, and Latin-Americans as member churches has called this narrow theological understanding of the church into question. It is not that Third World Christians reject the christological focus of the WCC. On the contrary, they insist that the christological confession of the WCC must be validated by a political commitment that is necessitated by it. In the Christologies of Asian, African, and Latin-American liberation theologies,[18] Jesus Christ is defined not so much with the substance language of Greek philosophy as found in the Nicean and Chalcedonian definitions of 325 and 451. For many Third World theologians, Jesus is the Liberator[19] who came, as the Gospel of Luke says,

> to bring the good news to the poor,
> to proclaim liberty to captives
> and to the blind new sight,
> to set the downtrodden free,
> to proclaim the Lord's year of favor. (4:18, JB)

The church is that people who have been called into being by the life, death, and resurrection of Jesus, so that they can bear witness to Jesus' lordship by participating with him in the struggle of freedom. This means that the primary definition of the church is not its confessional affirmations, but rather its political commitment on behalf of the poor.

To liberate the poor requires social analysis that explains the origin and nature of human poverty. Why are people poor, and who benefits from their poverty? This question places the church in the context of society and forces it to be self-critical as it seeks to realize its mission of bearing witness to God's rule that is coming in and through the human struggles to liberate the poor. The church bears witness to Christ's lordship not only in preaching about justice, but also in being the agent for its implementation in society.

The Church as the Servant of God's Coming Future

If Jesus Christ is Lord of the church, then the church is his servant. It is that congregation of people whose identity as the people of God arises from a definition of servanthood that is derived from Jesus' life, death, and resurrection. By definition, the church exists for others because its being is determined by the one who died on the cross for others.

The others for whom the church exists are the poor and not the rich, the downtrodden and oppressed and not the proud and the mighty. Because the church is a community called into being by the "Crucified God,"[20] it must be a crucified church, living under the cross.

The servanthood of the church is defined by the cross of Jesus and nowhere else. To be a servant of the crucified One is to be his representative in society, bearing witness to (in words, actions, and suffering body) the rule that Jesus revealed in his life, death, and resurrection. We must be careful not to spiritualize servanthood so as to camouflage its concrete, political embodiment. To be a servant of Jesus means more than meeting together every Sunday for worship and other liturgical gatherings. It means more than serving as an officer or even a pastor of a church. Servanthood includes a political component that thrusts a local congregation in society where it must take sides with the poor. Servanthood is a call to action that commits one in struggle for the poor.

Servanthood is the opposite of the world's definition of lordship. That was why Jesus said to his disciples:

> You know that among the pagans their so-called rulers lord it over them, and their great men make their authority felt. This

76

is not to happen among you. No; anyone who wants to become great among you must be your servant, and anyone who wants to be first among you must be slave to all. (Mark 10:42–44, JB)

The task of the church is more than preaching sermons about justice and praying for the liberation of all. The church must be the agent of justice and liberation about which it proclaims. A confessional affirmation of peace is not enough. The church must represent in its congregational life and seek to structure in society the peace about which it speaks. When a congregation does not even attempt to structure in its life and in the society the gospel that it preaches, why should anyone believe what it says? "To affirm that [people] are persons and as persons should be free, and yet do nothing tangible to make this affirmation a reality, is a farce."[21]

It is the cross of Jesus that connects the church with the victim. "We cannot speak of the death of Jesus until we speak of the real death of people," writes Gustavo Gutiérrez. Unnecessary starvation in Ethiopia, staggering poverty throughout the world, and rich American churches continue to sing and pray to Jesus as if the gospel has nothing to do with feeding the hungry and clothing the naked. In 1980 the World Bank reported that, "excluding China, approximately 750 million persons live in 'absolute poverty'" of which "40,000 small children die" each day "from malnutrition and infection."[22] All this is unnecessary. But we live in a nation that is more concerned about using food as "a tool in the kit of American diplomacy," to quote former secretary of agriculture Earl Butz, than using it to save the lives of starving human beings. The United States feeds people missiles. According to Arthur Simon, author of *Bread for the World:*

> In 1984 the United States devoured approximately $663 million each day in direct military spending—more than the entire annual budgets of the World Health Organization and the UN Development Program combined. The United States allocates about 40 times more for military defense than it does for development assistance.[23]

With so many people dying in the world, how can the churches continue their organizational routine and still expect sensitive people to believe that they are concerned about the cross of Jesus? That is why Hugo Assmann has said that "the church cannot be the reason for its own existence."[24] To preserve itself is to destroy itself. Nothing is more applicable to the church's identity than Jesus' claim that the person who would save his or her life shall lose it, and the person who loses his or her life "for my sake" shall find it. The church's distinctive identity is found not in itself, but in the crucified Jesus, whose Spirit calls the church into being for service on behalf of victimized people.

When the church makes its political commitment on behalf of the poor, the historical actions of the church bear witness to an ultimate hope that is grounded in the resurrection of Jesus. The church is a hoping community. It believes that the things that are can and ought to be otherwise. How is it possible to hope in hopeless situations? That is the question that all oppressed people must face when their projects of freedom end in failure? How can they believe that they are what they shall be when their history seems to be closed to the future?

It is in the historical context of an apparently closed future that Jesus Christ "makes a way out of no way" by creating a people who believe that because of his resurrection "that which is cannot be true." This is God's distinctive gift for the oppressed who otherwise would not have the courage to "keep on keeping on" even though the odds are against them. Max Weber has expressed this experience of the poor in sociological terms.

The sense of honor of disprivileged classes rests on some concealed promise for the future which implies the assignment of some function, mission, or vocation to them. What they cannot claim to *be*, they replace by the worth of that which they one day will *become*. . . . Their hunger for a worthiness that has not fallen their lot . . . produces this conception from which is derived the rationalistic idea of a providence, a significance in the eyes of some divine authority possessing a scale of values different from the one operating in the world of man.[25]

According to Weber, "since every need for salvation is an expression of some distress, social or economic oppression is an effective source of salvation beliefs."[26] Because the hope for salvation is always related to or derived from situations of distress, Weber has a different sociological evaluation of the religion of privileged classes.

> Other things being equal, classes with high social and economic privilege will scarcely be prone to evolve the idea of salvation. Rather they assign to religion the primary function of legitimizing their own life pattern or situation in the world. This universal phenomenon is rooted in a certain basic psychological pattern. When a man who is happy compares his position with that of one who is unhappy, he is not content with the fact of his happiness, the consciousness that he has earned his good fortune, in contrast to the unfortunate one who must equally have earned his misfortune. Our everyday experience proves that there exists just such a psychological need for reassurance as to the legitimacy or deservedness of one's happiness, whether this involves political success, superior economic status, . . . or anything else. What the privileged classes require of religion, if anything at all, is this psychological reassurance of legitimacy.[27]

"Correspondingly different," according to Weber, "is the situation of the disprivileged. Their particular need is release from suffering."[28] They look forward to the time when the things that are no longer will be. Because there is so little in their history that reflects their humanity, they are forced by the unrealized vision in their historical struggle to look beyond history in the hope that the truth which is not present in their situation will soon take place in God's eschatological future. This eschatological hope of the oppressed is not an opiate or a sedative, because it is a hope derived from struggle and never separated from it. God is the power who transforms the suffering of the present into hope for the future. That is why religious ecstasy, with shouts of praise and bodily rhythm, characterizes the worship style of the oppressed. Through sermon, song, prayer, and testimony they describe another realm of experience that they believe will be the decisive statement about their humanity. No people have expressed this eschatological hope with greater depth of apocalyptic imagination than black slaves in North America. "Where shall I be when the first trumpet soun'; soun' so loud till it woke up de dead." "One day, one day 'bout twelve o'clock, O this ol' earth goin' reel an' rock." "O my Lord, what a mornin', when de stars begin to fall!" "When de sun refuse to shine, when de moon goes down in blood!" "In dat great gettin' up mornin'," "de worl' will be on fire," and "you'll see de stars a-fallin', de forked lightin', de coffins burstin', and de righteous marchin'." "De dumb will talk, de lame will walk, de blind will see, and de deaf will hear."

CHAPTER 5

The Service of Theology to the Servant Task of Pastoral Ministry

Schubert M. Ogden

THE GENERAL TOPIC OF THIS ESSAY, LIKE THE OTHERS IN this book, is the pastoral ministry of the church and, more specifically, the servant task of pastoral ministry. But there are two points at which this discussion differs from that of the other contributors. First, its special topic is the service of theology to the servant task of the church's ministry. Although there is general agreement that theology performs an essential service to pastoral ministry, there has long been, and continues to be, considerable disagreement as to just how this service is to be understood and performed. Assuming, then, that the service of theology is also essential to pastoral ministry's servant task, one cannot understand this task without understanding how theology properly serves it. This means, of course, that none of the other contributors will be able to discuss his special topic without implicitly discussing the service of theology. But from all appearances, none discusses this

Schubert M. Ogden, Ph.D., is University Distinguished Professor of Theology, Southern Methodist University, Dallas, Texas.

topic explicitly, while it is precisely this that I have the responsibility to do.

Second, mine is a discussion in systematic theology rather than in historical or practical theology. Since one of the things that will have to be done in the course of the inquiry is to clarify just what it is that distinguishes such discussion, there is no need to go into that now. Suffice it to say that one of the questions that systematic theology has the task of answering is the question about the nature and task of theology itself. Of course, both historical and practical theology have contributions to make toward answering this as much as any other theological question. But to ask, as I propose to do, how theology properly serves the servant task of pastoral ministry is to ask the kind of question that systematic theology is required to answer.

The Scope of the Question

With this much by way of introduction, let me proceed to my initial task, which is to clarify the scope of the question, given the terms in which the general topic of this book has been formulated. Such clarification is necessary because both these terms are ambiguous in that each can be reasonably taken in more than one sense.

Consider, first, the pastoral ministry of the church, which is doubly ambiguous taken simply in itself. It is ambiguous in one way because it can mean either (1) the general ministry that is constitutive of the visible church and to which, therefore, all Christians are called, or (2) the special ministry that, being constituted by the visible church, is representative of it and to which, therefore, only some Christians are called. But the term is ambiguous in yet another way in that it can mean either (1) the special ministry of the visible church in all its forms or (2) one particular form of the special ministry. Thus, even when it is taken alone, the pastoral ministry of the church has at least three senses that can and should be distinguished, namely, those in which it can mean either (1) the general ministry of the visible church, (2) the special ministry of the visible church in all its forms, or (3) one particular form of special ministry, which I shall refer to hereafter as a specialized ministry.

The servant task of pastoral ministry involves still more ambiguity because of the different things that can also be understood by "the servant task." What lies behind this term, obviously, is the well-known christological distinction according to which the work of Christ is interpreted in terms of the Old Testament offices of "prophet," "priest," and "king." Depending on how one construes these terms, one can take them or their cognate adjectives either as designating three tasks of Christ's work or as three metaphors for understanding its one and only task. Applied to the visible church, then, talk of Christ's work as king becomes talk of the church's work as servant, while still allowing for both of these interpretations. Thus, the servant task of the church's ministry can mean either (1) one of its tasks among others properly spoken of as its "servant" task as distinct from its "priestly" and "prophetic" tasks; or (2) its one and only task understood in terms of the mataphor of "servant" rather than the other metaphors of "priest" and "prophet."

Taking all of these ambiguities into account, we may say that the servant task of pastoral ministry has at least six senses in which it can mean either (1) the one task of the general ministry of the visible church; (2) one among other tasks of the general ministry; (3) the one task of the special ministry of the visible church; (4) one among other tasks of the special ministry; (5) the one task of a specialized ministry of the visible church; or (6) one among other tasks of this specialized ministry. To ask, then, about the service of theology to the servant task of pastoral ministry is to ask a question whose scope covers at least six questions, ranging all the way from the first

83

and most general sense of the terms in which it is formulated to the last and most specific sense of these terms. It will be well to keep this in mind throughout the discussion, since I shall not pursue the question in the different senses in which it might be pursued. And this is true even though, as I now hope to show, the different senses of the terms can all be seen to be deeply united once the key term ministry is understood to have the meaning that properly belongs to it.

Ministry as Witness

My proposal for understanding "ministry" is that it be interpreted in terms of "witness" and, more exactly, "the act of witnessing." In making this proposal, I am following up two lines of reflection that together seem naturally to lead to it.

The first originates in the exegesis of Paul's statement about ministry in 2 Corinthians 5:18f. This is the statement that God "gave us [which is to say, each and every Christian] the ministry of reconciliation." What is striking about this statement is that it is closely related to, indeed, coordinate with, two other statements that Paul makes in these same verses, namely, that God "has reconciled us to himself through Christ" and "has established among us the word of reconciliation."[1] Clearly, the two phrases, "the *ministry* of reconciliation" and "the *word* of reconciliation," are to be interpreted in terms of each other as both referring to the means instituted by God whereby through Christians the event of reconciliation is again and again made present or re-presented. Insofar, then, as they are not simply two ways of saying the same thing, they serve to bring out two distinguishable moments of the one process of re-presenting this event.

At this point the other line of reflection converges with the first. It begins with the realization that the term witness is systematically ambiguous in much the same way as the term tradition and may therefore be analyzed by a parallel analysis.

Just as *traditio* has been understood to mean both *actus tradendi,* or "the act of traditioning," and *traditum tradendum,* or "the tradition being traditioned," so "witness" can be understood to mean both the *that* of witness, in the sense of the act of witnessing, and the *what* of witness, in the sense of the content it conveys either explicitly or by implication.[2] In the light of this analysis, the thought naturally suggests itself that it is precisely these two moments of witness that are brought out by Paul's distinction between "the ministry" and "the word" of reconciliation. In that case, to be guided in one's understanding of ministry by his statement about it is to interpret it as the act of witnessing, as distinct from the content of witness that he distinguishes by speaking of "the word."

Of course, in proposing that we so interpret it, I am as concerned as Paul is that we recognize the interdependence of these two moments even as we distinguish between them. Just as, in his view, the ministry of reconciliation both depends on and in turn is depended on by the word of reconciliation, so, in my view, the same is true of the act of witnessing and the content of witness. Indeed, one of the gains in interpreting Paul's statement by the single term witness is that the interdependence of these two moments becomes all the more evident.

But there is another thing about the term that is of the utmost importance to my proposal to use it. It not only allows for, but also requires the distinction between *explicit* and *implicit* witness. Obviously, the sense of "witness" in this entire discussion is the sense it has as a shorthand expression for "the Christian witness of faith." So understood, it refers simply to the expression of Christian faith through words and deeds that are at once from faith and for faith, in that they both arise out of the self-understanding in which faith consists, and are directed toward the same self-understanding. But just as self-understanding in general necessarily finds

85

expression through the whole of human praxis and culture, so the self-understanding of Christian faith cannot but be expressed through all that a Christian says and does, secular as well as religious. Even so, there is a difference between the religious and the secular insofar as religion expresses explicitly the self-understanding that everything secular expresses only implicitly. Because of this difference, Christian faith, also, must always find expression not only explicitly through religion, but also implicitly through all the secular forms of praxis and culture. This explains why the "witness" in terms of which "ministry" is to be interpreted can and must be understood as both *explicit* and *implicit* witness.

Given this understanding, however, I am in a position to interpret all the different senses of the terms in which the question is formulated as well as to recognize the profound unity between them. If the one task of ministry in any of its senses is properly understood as the task of witnessing, then by the servant task of pastoral ministry in the first, third, and fifth senses previously clarified is meant just this task of witnessing both explicitly and implicitly as general, special, and specialized ministry, respectively. This assumes that such a task is appropriately understood in terms of the biblical metaphor of "servant." On the one hand this assumption is surely warranted if explicit and implicit witness together exhaust the ways of serving God by serving those of whom God has always already become the servant. On the other hand, explicit and implict witness are different, and there are good reasons for understanding the task of witnessing explicitly in terms of the other metaphors of priest and prophet, leaving servant to interpret the task of witnessing implicitly only. In that case the servant task of pastoral ministry would need to be taken in either the second, fourth, or sixth sense of the terms and interpreted to mean the task of witnessing implicitly only as either general, special, or specialized ministry.

On this interpretation the servant task of pastoral ministry ranges in meaning between two different but deeply united tasks of witnessing. In its first and most general sense it means the task of witnessing both explicitly and implicitly that belongs to the general ministry of the church and is, therefore, the responsibility of each and every Christian. In my view, this is also its foundational sense, for not only does it include both explicit and implicit witness, but it also refers to the most basic level of such witness, which is alone constitutive of the visible church. By contrast, in its sixth and most specific sense it means that the task of witnessing implicitly belongs only to the special ministry of the church in one of its particular forms and is, therefore, the responsibility solely of the relatively few Christians called to such ministry. This, I take it, is the sense illustrated by the specialized ministry usually called pastoral counseling. At any rate, in my view, such a ministry is specialized not only by being concerned with the particular needs of individual persons, but also by being addressed to such of these needs as cannot be met except by implicit witness.

Theology as Critical Reflection on Witness

This brings me to the central task of understanding the other main term in which the question is formulated, namely, theology. In my judgment, the easiest way to achieve such understanding is to look more closely at the act of witnessing meant by "ministry" in the several senses of the term.

From the standpoint of contemporary philosophical analysis, the act of witnessing is one among the large number of acts that human beings typically perform that are generically described as "speech acts."[3] Thus, it is in important respects like such other more or less different acts as making statements, issuing commands, and making promises. One such respect is the characteristic double structure it involves, of which we already took notice when we distinguished between the act of witnessing and the content of witness on which it depends.[4] Another respect in which it is like other speech acts is that it, too, may be performed and yet need not be performed by performing a language act, which is to say, an act of uttering certain words. As true as it is that having language enables one to perform the act of witnessing with greater ease and clarity about one's intention than would otherwise be possible, one may nevertheless perform it without uttering any words at all, just as one can issue a command to close the door by waving one's arm or promise to be faithful to one's spouse by giving a kiss.[5]

The act of witnessing is like other speech acts, above all, in that it expresses or implies certain claims to validity. For my purposes here, it is sufficient to focus on the two claims that are specific to witnessing as such.

By virtue of the characteristic double structure it involves, any act of witnessing is both an explication or implication of the content of witness and a specification of the act of witnessing in terms of some particular situation. Correspondingly, any such act expresses or implies the claim to be both adequate to its content and fitting to its situation. For the most part, these two claims to validity are made only implicitly simply by the act of witnessing itself. But in certain special cases, such as the formal definition of what is to count as normative witness, the claims to be adequate to the content of witness as well as fitting to the situation may be made quite explicitly. In either case, the making of the two claims is entirely of a piece with the act of witnessing, since it cannot be performed except by somehow making them.

The difficulty, however, is that both claims may be invalid insofar as any act of witnessing may always fail to be either adequate or fitting. Furthermore, both claims can be rendered problematic in a given case as soon as there is any other act of witnessing either already performed or in prospect that is sufficiently different from the first that the claims of both acts logically cannot be valid claims. But this, obviously, is precisely the situation that at least appears to develop, given a plurality of acts of witnessing. On the face of it, the validity claims expressed or implied by one such act are invalidated by the corresponding claims of another contrary one.

This is particularly clear in the case of the claim that an act of witnessing is adequate to its content. The content of witness is explicitly formulated in some terms or other in what I call "the constitutive christological assertion," which is classically formulated in the assertion "Jesus is the Christ" and can be formulated today by asserting that Jesus is the decisive representation of the meaning of ultimate reality for us.[6] In the nature of the case, the claim of any act of witnessing to be adequate to this content is a twofold claim: on the one hand, it is the claim that the act in question is appropriate to the christological assertion because it is in agreement with normative Christian witness; on the other hand, it is the claim that the act in question is credible to human existence because it is in agreement with common human experience. But, obviously, both of these claims are and must be radically problematic, given the actual plurality of acts of witnessing and the still greater plurality of alternative answers to the existential question about the meaning of ultimate reality.

Not only are there contrary acts of witnessing not all of which can be appropriate to their content, but there is also no agreement among Christians about what is to count as normative witness. While Protestants have traditionally appealed to "scripture alone" against the classic Roman Catholic principle of "scripture and tradition," revisionary believers and theologians in both communions have increasingly looked to "the historical Jesus" as the real Christian norm. But if this means that no claim to appropriateness can be anything but radically problematic, the same is even more obviously true of any claim to credibility. Once we recognize, as we must, that the Christian witness, in all its forms, represents but one among a number of contrary faiths and ideologies whereby human beings have sought to come to terms with their existence, we cannot deny that the claim of any act of witnessing to be credible is extremely hard to validate. It could not be otherwise, considering that there certainly is no agreement among human beings generally about the standards of meaning and truth that are given implicitly in common human experience.

There is one further respect in which the act of witnessing is like other speech acts. Once the claims to validity that it necessarily involves have been rendered problematic, there is nothing to be done if it is still to be performed except to validate its claims by way of critical reflection. The reason for this is that one cannot make such claims in good faith except by assuming the obligation to validate them if and when they are seriously questioned.[7] Consequently, to perform the act of witnessing obligates one to give reasons for its claims to be both adequate to its content, and so credible as well as appropriate, and fitting to its situation. My contention is that what is properly meant by "theology" is either the process or the product of giving such reasons. In this sense I define theology in the context of this discussion as critical reflection on the witness that in turn is the meaning of ministry.

Of course, this is not the only sense in which the term theology may be understood. If one is guided simply by the literal meaning of the word, "theology" is *logos* about *theos,* and so thought and speech about God. But if "theology" is taken sufficiently broadly to mean all thought and speech about God, it is simply another word for what I have been calling "witness," or, more exactly, "the content of witness" as distinct from the act of witnessing. I readily allow that there is clear precedent in tradition for using "theology" in such a broad sense, and I have no objection to its still being so used. Even so, there is also clear precedent for using the term more strictly, in something like the sense I have been trying to distinguish. So used, it no longer means all thought and speech about God, but only such as are involved in either the process or the product of critically reflecting on such thought and speech as well as the action through which faith also finds expression. In any event, the critical point is the difference in principle between *making* validity claims, as one does in performing the act of witnessing, and *critically reflecting* on such claims, as one does in engaging in what I, at least, take "theology" properly to mean. However this difference is expressed, it is what has to be understood if what I mean by "the service of theology to the servant task of pastoral ministry" is to be understood. For that service, quite simply, is the service of reflecting sufficiently critically on the validity claims expressed or implied in carrying out this servant task to be able to validate these claims.

Before inquiring further as to the precise character of this service, I want to develop the understanding of theology that I have proposed by making two comments: first, on how it allows for the division of theology into the three main disciplines of systematic, practical, and historical theology; and second, on the account it requires of the relation of theology to other secular forms of critical reflection.

It will be clear from what has been said that an act of witnessing is constituted as such only by the content of witness on which it depends. Except for this content, the act neither would nor could be the act of bearing the Christian witness of faith that I have consistently supposed the term witness to mean. This implies, among other things, that no question about the validity of the claim of witness to be fitting to its situation would even arise but for its other claim to be adequate to its content and, therefore, both appropriate and credible. Accordingly, the constitutive question of theology, in the sense of the question that constitutes it as critical reflection on the validity claims expressed or implied by witness, must be the question about the validity of this other claim to adequacy. Once this question is asked, the process of theological reflection is under way. On the contrary, until this question is asked, theological reflection has not begun.

At the same time, the question about the validity of the

claim of witness to be adequate to its content, and hence appropriate and credible, is not the only question theology must ask. Aside from the fact that any act of witnessing also makes the claim to be fitting to its situation, thereby allowing for the question about the validity of this claim, the claim of witness to be appropriate cannot be validated except by asking yet another theological question. If this claim means, as we have seen, that the witness in question is in agreement with normative Christian witness, it can be established as valid only by first determining what is to count as normative witness. But since normative witness must be just as much a matter of history as any other Christian witness, what is to count as such can be determined only by asking a properly historical kind of question.

So it is that the understanding of theology for which I have argued allows for its asking not only its constitutive question about the validity of the claim of witness to be adequate to its content, but also the two further questions about the validity of its claim to be fitting to its situation and about what is to count as the normative witness by which its claim to be appropriate can alone be validated. But this means, I submit, that this understanding of theology allows for its division into the three main disciplines of systematic, practical, and historical theology, which have the responsibilities, respectively, of asking these three questions.

This leads to the second comment about the account this understanding requires of theology's relation to other secular forms of critical reflection. The essential point here is that, although theology is critical reflection on witness, and therefore irreducibly different from every other form of reflection, it is nevertheless related to these other forms and dependent on them. Thus, historical theology necessarily depends on historical reflection generally as well as on the various special sciences, natural and human, on which history in turn is itself dependent. Likewise, practical theology is essentially dependent on all the secular forms of reflection on praxis for critically understanding the particular situation of witness, its possibilities and limitations. So, too, systematic theology necessarily depends on philosophical theology and secular philosophy in general in order to validate the claim of witness to be credible because it is in agreement with common human experience that it is the proper business of philosophy to understand. In sum: theology can perform its own distinctive service only by depending on the service of these other forms of critical reflection. Moreover, the whole value of their service turns on their being precisely secular forms of reflection that are therefore independent of theology.

The Service of Theology as Indirect Service

The point I now wish to make is that there must be an analogous relation in turn between theology and the servant task of pastoral ministry. If theology is properly understood as critical reflection on witness, it must be, in its own way, independent of the witness on which it reflects. For this reason the service of theology about which we are asking cannot be direct, but only indirect, service.

This contention may scarcely seem controversial as long as "theology" is understood in the narrow sense in which we often take it. Given the specialization of roles and functions long since institutionalized in our society and culture, it may seem only natural to think and speak of theology simply as academic theology, which is to say, the process of critically reflecting on witness carried on by certain specialists whose expertise at once requires and makes possible a correspondingly specialized form of higher education. Because academic theology, in this sense, is indeed only indirectly related to the task of witnessing as it, for its part, is normally institutionalized, the claim that theology's service to this task is indirect only may seem too obvious to be worth making. But this is not the sense—at least, not the only sense—that I have allowed to the term theology. On the contrary, I have proposed that it be understood essentially simply as the process of critical reflection required to validate the claims of witness to be both adequate to its content and fitting to its situation. Therefore, while I readily agree that this process can and should be carried on at a professional level and in an academic form, I should no more think to restrict it to this level or form than I should suppose that the special ministry of the church is the only level of its pastoral ministry. Indeed, the most basic level of theology, exactly like the most basic level of ministry, is lay rather than professional. It belongs not only to some Christians, but to all Christians to reflect critically on the claims to validity that are expressed or implied by the act of witnessing.

My point, however, is that even at this most basic lay level, the service of theology can only be indirect. Precisely because it is just such critical reflection, not because it happens to be carried on by professionals or academics, it differs in principle from the witness on which it reflects and, therefore, can serve this witness only indirectly.

But this, clearly, is far from being a noncontroversial point. In fact, today, even as throughout most of Christian history, theology is generally understood and performed as direct service to the task of witnessing. This is evident from the fact that even academic theologians are all but universally expected to be Christian believers and to carry on their reflection within the limits set by normative Christian witness.

To be sure, these expectations do not come to exactly the same thing in the different contexts in which theology can be carried on because, as I noted earlier, there is no agreement among Christians about what is to count as normative witness. If in a traditional Roman Catholic context, it is scripture and tradition; if in a traditional Protestant context, it is scripture alone. Correspondingly, the Catholic theologian is typically expected to believe and reflect within the one institutional church whose magisterium alone has the authority to interpret the scriptural witness, while the Protestant theologian is typically expected to believe and reflect within the one visible church that is always more or less visible in all the institutional churches but is never to be identified with any of them. Notwithstanding this important difference, however, theologians in both contexts are evidently expected to perform the same kind of direct service to the task of witnessing. Nor is it otherwise with theologians who carry on their reflection in a revisionary rather than a traditional context, in which the norm of Christian witness is neither scripture and tradition nor scripture alone, but the historical Jesus. However Jesus may be understood in such a context, whether as the moral and religious teacher of an earlier liberal theology or as the more radical figure of contemporary political theology and theology of liberation, theology is understood to be possible at all only on the basis of a prior commitment to Jesus' cause.

There are reasons, naturally, why this way of understanding and performing theology should be so long established and widely shared. No doubt most academic theologians are, in some sense, Christian believers, if only because anyone who was not would hardly be motivated to assume the task. Moreover, whether or not one has to be a Christian to do theology, one evidently has to do theology to be a Christian. This is so, at any rate, if every Christian is called to the general ministry of witnessing and, therefore, to bearing a witness that is valid according to its own, at least, implicit claims to validity. For, clearly, the only way to validate these claims is by the process of critical reflection that is properly called "theology." Furthermore, it lies in the nature of the decision of faith to accept the truth of Christian witness and, therefore, to believe that any witness that is appropriate because it is in agreement with what is normatively Christian must by that very fact also be credible because it is in agreement with what is commonly experienced. Consequently, from the standpoint of Christian believers, there is a certain logic to expecting theologians to carry on their reflection within the limits set by normative witness. Finally, we ought not to forget the ambiguity of the term theology, which in one of its senses, as has been seen, is equivalent simply to "witness." Considering, then, that witness indeed ought to be performed on the basis of a prior commitment to what is normatively Christian, one may be misled into supposing that the same is true of the critical reflection on the validity of witness that is also meant by "theology."

Whatever the reasons for it, however, this conventional alternative against which I am arguing is open to a fatal objection. To the precise degree to which it understands and performs theology as direct service to the act of witnessing, it is forced to deny the essential nature and task of theology as critical reflection. I do not mean by this, obviously, that its denial has to be explicit or that those who opt for it may not continue to think and speak of theology as "critical reflection." My point, rather, is strictly logical: whatever it may be called, being reflection that is of direct service to witness just because it is done by believers within the limits of normative witness precludes theology's also being reflection that is critical only because it does not assume the validity of any of the claims that witness expresses or implies, but rather questions the validity of all of them.

Of course, it is also only logical to recognize that the claim of any witness to be appropriate can be validated only by testing its agreement with some witness taken to be normative. But aside from the fact that, given the plurality of positions previously referred to, what is taken as normative must itself be problematic, whether or not the other claim of witness to be credible is also a valid claim can never be settled simply by appealing to normative witness. There always remains the question of the credibility of normative witness; and if believers as such must indeed claim its credibility, the validity of their claim can never be validated by a process of reflection that directly serves their witness and, therefore, cannot even begin without already assuming its validity.

On the contrary, any process of reflection sufficiently critical to be able to validate this claim as well as the other claims of witness to be appropriate and fitting can be of service to it only indirectly. This, if you will, is the price that must always be paid for critical reflection if it is the genuine article. It can validate the claims on which it reflects only insofar as it is sufficiently independent also to invalidate them. Consequently, if theology is properly understood as critical reflection on witness, it must be independent enough to invalidate the claims to validity that witness expresses or implies. But, then, the only service theology can possibly perform to the servant task of a ministry whose whole meaning is witness is the indirect service allowed for by this kind of independence.

The Theologian as *Servus Servorum Dei*

Indirect as it must be, however, the service of theology to the servant task of pastoral ministry is nonetheless essential, and that precisely because it is indirect. That this is so should be clear enough from what has already been said. But any doubt about it can be removed by simply recalling the meanings we recognized in the term "the servant task."

Applied to the pastoral ministry, this term means either the task of witnessing both explicitly and implicitly at the general or special level or in a specialized form or else the task of witnessing implicitly only as general, special, or specialized ministry. In either case the task can be performed only by bearing a valid witness, a witness whose own, at least implicit, claims to be adequate to its content and fitting to its situation are valid claims. But, clearly, the only way to validate these claims is by just that process of critical reflection that is properly meant by "theology." It follows, therefore, that the

97

service that theology alone is able to provide is essential to the task of witnessing that is the servant task of pastoral ministry.

It is possible, naturally, that the need for theology's service may be less urgent in some situations than in others. As in the case of other speech acts, the validity claims expressed or implied by the act of witnessing may not have become problematic, or problematic enough to require moving to the level of critical reflection to validate them.[8] In that event the obligation assumed in making them can be discharged immediately, at the level of performing the act itself, simply by appealing to the standard practice of ministry and to normative witness or by invoking what is generally accepted as common human experience. As long as these procedures suffice to answer such questions as may arise about whether witness is fitting to its situation or adequate to its content, theology as such hardly seems necessary and may not be supposed to perform any essential service. But let the situation change enough so that questions persist even after following these procedures and the need for critical reflection if the act of witnessing is still to be performed becomes only too apparent. At the same time it becomes evident that the service of theology as alone able to provide such critical reflection is an essential service.

Another variable we need to recognize is that theology's service cannot be exactly the same to all the different tasks of witnessing that may be meant by "the servant task of pastoral ministry." Depending on the sense in which these terms are understood, theology, also, must be understood to have a somewhat different task. Thus, for example, in any of the three senses in which they mean the task of witnessing implicitly only, theology's service in critically reflecting on the adequacy of witness to its content will need to come primarily from that part of systematic theology that is properly distinguished as "moral theology" because it focuses attention on the expression of faith through action, secular as well as religious. Or, again, the service of theology as practical theology cannot be simply the same when it reflects on the fittingness of witness to its situation at the two levels of the general and the special ministry. But having recognized these as well as such other differences as may be relevant, we may still be confident that the service of theology is, after all, one. Because for all their differences, the different tasks of witnessing are deeply united, theology's service to each of them is the same essential service of validating their claims to be valid and thus to perform the servant task of pastoral ministry.

This all assumes, of course, that theology, in fact, provides this service of validation. But to avoid any misunderstanding, I should acknowledge that not everything that is called "theology" may actually go to validate the claims of witness to be both adequate and fitting. Here, too, theology is like other forms of critical reflection in that it may always go wrong not only in one direction, but in two. Not only may it be made to serve the task of witnessing so directly that it ceases to be critical reflection in more than name only, but it may also become so remotely related to what is really at stake in witnessing as no longer to be essential to validating the claims that are thereby expressed or implied.

For various reasons this second way of going wrong is particularly likely in the case of professional theology, especially when it is pursued in an academic context. Given the high degree of specialization not only of academic theology, but also of the other secular forms of reflection on which it depends, much of the work routinely done by theological specialists is hardly essential to validating the claims of witness. Moreover, academic theology is like any other highly developed field of reflection in generating its own inertias, which over time may make for a considerable gap between the theological questions being pursued by academic theologians and those that are most urgent to ministers of the church as well as other theologians who pursue their reflection in the church rather than in the academy. But there is another, still more fundamental reason why not only professional theology, but lay theology as well may no longer be essential to the task of witnessing. Before one can validate any claim to validity, one has to analyze accurately the kind of claim it actually is. Consequently, there is always a risk in any process of critical reflection, including theology, that one will confuse the claim one is supposed to validate with some other different kind of claim. But in that event all that one may proceed to do by way of giving reasons for the claim will be simply irrelevant to validating it.

No one acquainted with the modern history of theology will be a stranger to this confusion. But for it, the long and still continuing conflicts between religion and science and faith and history could never have arisen. The lesson to be learned from these conflicts, however, is, once again, that not everything that passes for theology is properly that—whether because it is not really critical reflection or, as in this case, because it is critical reflection on something other than the validity claims expressed or implied by the Christian witness. On the contrary, wherever theology is critical reflection, and critical reflection on precisely these claims, the service it performs to the task of bearing this witness could not be more essential.

Recognizing this, I do not hesitate to speak of the theologian as "servant of the servants of God." From at least the time of Gregory the Great, this title has been applied to the office of the Pope as primate of the universal church; and an appropriate title it is, considering the saying of Jesus in the Gospels that "if any one would be first, he must be last of all and servant of all [Mark 9:35]." It is applied just as appropriately, however, to any other office of the special ministry, if one holds, as I do, that the whole point of any such office is in one way or another to be of service to the servants of God who constitute the general ministry of the church. But if the argument of this essay is sound, the title is just as appropriate for the office of the theologian, lay, professional, and academic. Although in this case the service to God's servants is but the indirect service of critical reflection, it alone can make good their claims to fulfill their servant task.

CHAPTER 6

Plurality: Our New Situation

Langdon Gilkey

How can the church and its leaders be "servants" in a pluralistic environment? The word plural here refers to a religiously pluralistic world, a world of many and varied religions. What effect does such an environment have on the pastor?

The meaning of the present plural world signifies more than the merely plural. For there have always been many religions, and the churches have been more than aware of that fact. Hence I mean something different, something new; I refer to a new problem or an opportunity raised by plurality, that is, a new consciousness with regard to plurality. I suggest that this new consciousness entails a feeling of "rough parity," as well as diversity, between religions. And by parity I mean *at least* the presence of both truth and grace in "other ways." I shall assume that this is the common consciousness on this issue. This consciousness is new for the churches. From the earliest period, through the Patristics down to the liberals of the nineteenth and twentieth centuries, the absoluteness and

---

Langdon Gilkey, Ph.D., is Shailer Mathews Professor of Theology, Divinity School, University of Chicago, Chicago, Illinois.

superiority of the Christian faith were assumed without question. Even to consider "parity" with other religions is, therefore, a radically new departure. As a consequence, it represents a quite uncharted sea both for theology and for the life and attitudes of the churches.

The Causes of the New Situation

I begin by looking at some of the more important causes of this new situation. The theological causes stretch back into the liberal period, that is, back into the Enlightenment and its effects on theology. Two changes in theology have helped to usher in this new consciousness. Interestingly, although these changes occurred under the auspices of liberal theology, they retained their strength during the neoorthodox period and well into our own.

The first change is the renewed emphasis on *love*, rather than on "purity of faith." As Calvin puts this in the *Institutes*, this requirement takes precedence over that of loving one's neighbor; in effect, it is the defense of God and the name of God, and thus is a practical application of the first commandment. On this basis every Christian is required to struggle against, and even to eliminate, false doctrine and heresy wherever they appear. One need not cite the appalling results of this reading of Christian requirements in the baleful history of the churches. It was, therefore, no small matter when, with liberalism, the obligation of loving one's neighbor was seen as taking precedence over defending the purity of doctrine. As a result of this shift, the values of tolerance and of ecumenical fellowship—even among those who disagreed theologically—were changed in status. There were now true marks of the Christian spirit, replacing the dogmatic fervor and the intolerance of "blasphemy" that had characterized the earlier situation. One basis for the ecumenical movement among the churches was thus established.

The second basis for this new attitude toward other faiths

complements the first. It is a new sense of the *historicity* of all doctrinal and confessional statements. With this sense, which also arose under Enlightenment influence, each set of dogmas or doctrines was viewed as a *perspective* on a truth beyond all of them, a perspective reflecting the cultural and historical viewpoints of that group at that time. Thus, none of them is absolute; and while each contains important elements of the truth, none of them excludes the other completely. And together, as complementing one another, they contain *more* of the truth than does any one singly.

Out of these two new views of confessional doctrines—the primacy of love and the relativity of every doctrinal or dogmatic proposition—the ecumenical movement among Christians was born. An attitude not only of tolerance, but also of positive interest and concern appeared within differing positions in Christianity. The stage was clearly set, therefore, by the midtwentieth century for the new view of plurality among religious faiths and their communities. However, during all this ecumenical progress the assumption remained that Christianity represented the final and definitive form of religion, since its founding revelation was unique, *Einmalig*, and so, in its own way, absolute.

If this last remark is valid, then we Christians must move to causes other than theological ones if we are to understand how this new attitude among religions, an attitude of rough parity, has arisen. I suggest that these other sorts of causes arise from the cultural and the historical spheres in which fundamental changes were taking place during this period. These changes can be summed up as, first, the decline of the sense of Western superiority, on the one hand, and a new feeling, on the other hand, of the ambiguity of the major elements of Western culture.

The importance of the assumption of the superiority of Western culture for my subject cannot be overemphasized. This assumption was of long duration, running deep indeed, and it dominated every level of cultural life, from top to bottom. For well over four centuries (from the early 1500s to 1945) the West had no military, political, or economic rivals elsewhere on the globe. As a consequence, Western nations ruled everywhere without challenge—except from one another. History had seemingly disposed of the competitive power of other cultures, and thus it had validated thoroughly the Western claim to superiority.

This mastery, while at first most evident in the areas of science and technology, did not, however, stop there. On the contrary, it spilled over onto every level of life: democracy in politics; personal autonomy in family and marriage; equality of men and women (the West thought itself farther along here than it was!); humanitarianism in ethics; and, of course, to crown it all, Christianity in religion. On each of these levels, from bottom to top, the West was clearly (in its own eyes and to many in other cultures) superior. This combination of military and economic mastery plus a presumed spiritual supremacy is devastatingly powerful, breeding in Westerners easy assumptions of the absoluteness of their own culture and of the irrelevance, if not primitivism, of the cultures of others that are to us now both odious and incredible. (See, as example of these attitudes, the two films *Gandhi* and *A Passage to India*.) It was also assumed without question that the underdeveloped cultures of the rest of the world would quickly transform themselves into latter-day copies of ourselves— since clearly progress for them, as for us, lay in becoming Western. The reality of this domination and the assumption of this superiority lasted until the end of World War II. Then all this changed with lightning rapidity.

In the 1970s and 1980s the effects of this change have begun to be felt, if not yet articulated. Militarily and politically, the vast empires of the West have vanished. The direct rule of the West is thus shrunken into its own borders. As a culture, its rule no longer spreads across the globe. Other centers of power now manifest themselves as possessing genuine parity, if not yet equality. Correspondingly, other cultural alternatives, other ways of life, have appeared as real options: from the older cultures of Asia, from diverse Communist experiments, from the societies of the so-called Third World. A pluralism, including a plurality of military and economic powers *and* of cultural perspectives, dominates our common world scene as never before.

As part of this same process, the institutions and goals of Western life seem neither as permanent nor as beneficent as they once did. For example, the Western autonomous family, once the ideal for most of Asia, now seems ambiguous at best, riven with divorce rates and threatened with transience. The future of Western society itself appears less the goal of history and more precarious. Those elements that once made it clearly superior—science, technology, and industrialism—now, on the contrary, create its own deepest dilemmas. They even threaten its continued life. Thus, instead of representing a clear progress, Western institutions now appear, at home and abroad, as deeply ambiguous; creative, alluring, but possibly lethal and (not irrelevantly) oppressive. The assumed superiority of the West has dissolved into a new pluralism and a new ambiguity, a new sense of parity among cultures and among alternative ways of life, and a new sense of the precariousness and even the menace of our own. The modern sense of change has itself changed. From one of buoyantly anticipating changes *in* Western culture, the sense of change has shifted to the more ominous feeling that changes will be *from* Western culture into something as yet unknown.

The present-day consequences of this process of change that I have rehearsed are directly relevant to my subject, the appearance of religious plurality. The first is the deeply felt malaise or anxiety about Western life and its prospects that pervades much of our society. This is not articulated widely, but it is there and its effects are everywhere: in the efforts to retrieve former values; in the return to a conservative posture;

in the pathological fear of seeming weak ("a paper tiger," as Nixon put it); in the certainty that the beliefs and norms that "made us great" are being lost. In all this we see a spiritual situation of deep uncertainty and anxiety, a situation ripe, as history shows, for the upsurge of religion. Correspondingly, the same situation is evident in the sudden and pervasive appearance of new religious cults and movements: some conservative, even fanatical, forms of traditional religious groups; some importations from Asiatic religions; some new, home-grown religious cults. The tide of the missionary enterprise has reversed itself, and the flow is now in exactly the opposite direction. It flows into a spiritually barren and anxious Western culture, not out of it into the rest of the world. Here, then, is a quite direct source for the new sense of the parity of religions, namely, the experience of their effective appearance, in power among us, on our turf!

It is then in terms of this new global setting that we can understand the appearance of a new attitude toward other religions, the attitude of parity. Western dominance, both political and spiritual, is quite gone. Western culture finds itself unsure of its own foundations and anxious about its future. New religious movements reflecting different religious viewpoints from traditional Western ones begin to appear with power among us, converting our friends—and frequently our children—and offering to us insights and practices that we both need and yet do not find at home.

It is in this context that dialogue among diverse religious traditions becomes a primary interest, indeed a need, for many to whom formerly relations with other traditions had been purely cursory, a polite but fleeting contact at best. Dialogue presupposes that each partner recognizes the other as, in some significant measure, equal, the bearer of a truth and a grace not possessed by oneself. Dialogue is, therefore, perhaps the clearest indicator of the new situation that we are analyzing, as it is also the most interesting new factor on the theological scene.

107

Christian Failings Revealed in the New Situation:
A Spiritual Vacuum

The new task of the Christian church is to uncover some of the important consequences for the life of the local church and for its leader, the pastor, in this new situation. What does it mean to be a *servant*, or the *servant church*, under these conditions? The Christian community is now the native ground for powerful mission movements representing alien and yet attractive religious alternatives—far more fascinating than other rival denominations!—and thus threatening us in a quite new way with the loss of members. How can the church react creatively rather than defensively to this new situation?

It is, of course, natural that the reaction of Christians be defensive and negative. The growing impact of non-Christian religions does represent a genuine threat to the stability of many congregations and families—as the numbers of former Protestants, Catholics, and Jews among each of the new religious movements (new to Christian communities) show. It is, however, both more creative and more accurate to react positively to this challenge, to welcome it as an opportunity, and to take full advantage of the possibilities for spiritual growth that it unquestionably offers. This attitude is not just a whistle in the dark. It is undeniable historically that many religious movements in India, China, and Japan, to take only three examples, were effectively revitalized by the challenge of Christian missions. One can clearly trace the changes that the power and influence of the new Christian groups effected in these religions, forcing them to new levels of self-understanding and perhaps especially to new ways of relating themselves to their world. Part, although not all, of the new power of these movements in the present—of Vedanta, Sikh, Yoga and Zen mission groups—derives from this vigorous *reaction* to the impingement of Christianity on them during the past century and a half. Correspondingly, from them, and from the necessities of our reaction to them, we may discover new emphases, new vitality, new methods.

One of the ways in which such reassessment and revitalization occur is through the uncovering of the weaknesses and lacks of the Christian community. Alternative forms of religion throw a sharp and critical light on older, taken-for-granted forms. Powerful options, offering much that we do not, reveal precisely where we fall short. Their presence thus not only impels us to change, but also shows us many of the most important directions of change. My own experience within both Sikh and Zen groups, here and in Japan, leads me to suggest that the weaknesses that they help to uncover in our own parish life center around the area of "spirituality," the *practice* of religion and so the direct *experiencing* of the holy. It is on that assumption that the following remarks are based, and it is in its light that my suggestions for the growth of the servant church and the servant pastorate are made.

It has long been noted that American churches have been suffering from a loss of powerful and meaningful public liturgy. It is not my purpose here to argue this point or trace out its multiple historical roots. It is sufficient to agree, as most would, that a sense of the holy does not pervade most of our present Sunday worship. Long before questions about the absence of God arose theologically, an awareness of that absence was present in many of our church services: hymns were sung, prayers were said, sermons preached. But anything more than that, any sacral presence to which the response of worship was being made, was unfelt and unknown. Strangely—and here the psychology and sociology of religion might help us—this lack seems particularly characteristic of the middle-class, bourgeois churches that represent mainline Protestant, and increasingly present Catholic, congregations. The same problem did not and does not arise in "gospel" churches, in which the Spirit always makes itself known as it did not in traditional Catholicism, in which the presence of the holy in sacramental liturgy was assumed. In both, the reality of the holy was directly apprehended, and worship, whatever its form, was experienced as a *response* to that felt

109

real presence. Contemporary worship, however, has few traces left of this presence or of the sense of the reality of the divine that is addressed.

Possibly it would be disturbing to most modern congregations—to most of *us*—if the holy *were* there. It might appear unmannerly, archaic, superstitious, fanatical (as many Christians tend to regard both "gospel" worship and traditional sacramental realism). One can think of many ways in which Christians would seek to evade it, for it would threaten, probably, our sense of what is real and what is appropriate. Yet it is undeniable that we seek for it and long for it. In the ways in which Christians tend to speak *theologically* about both sacrament and proclamation, we show that we *must* think of them in the terms of divine activity and presence, rather than in terms of human works, human signs. Thus, our theologies of liturgy soar higher than our experience of it, which remains generally earthbound, listening to a passable sermon and sharing in a meaningful rite. In any case much of our present church life is more barren liturgically and in its communal experiences of the divine than it is void in profundity of theological or ethical reflection.

Far sharper, however, is the crisis within the area of *personal* religious life. It is, of course, difficult to accumulate data in such regions, but one can talk with friends and colleagues and one can commune with oneself. Hypotheses in this area are, therefore, not so much the result of objective surveys as of reflection on small but still relevant ranges of experiences. And numerous conversations with those who have recently moved out of church life into membership within one of the newer sects validate over and over what these experiences intimate.

There is within the life of contemporary churches a vacuum within the area of spirituality, a vanishing of the habits and the rewards of personal piety. This is a vacuum that seems to balance and feed the emptiness of common worship referred to earlier. This is not the fault of Protestantism as such—as some are inclined to believe. First in Puritanism, then in Lutheran pietism, and certainly within the personal habits of "sectarian" Protestant groups, there was a rich tradition of personal piety: of regular Bible reading, personal prayer life, family worship, obedience to set rules governing all of life. These firm and all-encompassing habits or practices kept the daily lives of ordinary people in the closest touch with the holy. It was because of this daily communion with the sacred that Protestant individuals could come together in common worship and jointly commune with the holy—even in the most barren of liturgical structures. It is noteworthy that these habits of personal devotions and discipline lasted long after their orthodox theological background began to be criticized and revised, that is, well into the first half of the twentieth century. Even though the pastor's house in which I grew up was theologically and ethically "liberal," still I can well recall my father's daily devotions, his regular period by himself of Bible reading, and the family prayers that were taken for granted in our home. Although he had broken radically with traditional Protestant orthodoxy in theology, in his reading of the scriptures and in his commitment to the social gospel, his habits of personal piety remained a steady inheritance from that older world.

Now my point is that much if not all of this vanished, as did the prayer meetings in the Protestant churches, during the middle years of this century. Few of the neoorthodox generation, whatever their devotion to the evangelical gospel or to liberation in the world, were able to continue these habits of life, this life-style of personal piety and discipline. The causes of this are multiple and need not concern us here. Suffice it to say that even deeper than the vacuum in current worship is that in the area of personal piety and devotion. Faith and obedience are thus largely inward, within consciousness, on the one hand, and ethical, in actions within the world's life, on the other hand. In that central region of the self's *experiencing*—of itself, of the Word, of God's address to the self—there

111

is all too little going on. It is, moreover, hard for those who note and regret this situation to return to the evangelical personal piety of the end of the past century. There is little, in other words, that such Christians "do"—except attendance at church and their ethical actions within the world—in the task of embodying and nurturing their faith. Inwardness, sheer inwardness, rules; and as Kierkegaard, the apostle of inwardness, noted, inwardness without significant external embodiment can easily slip away.

What does all this have to do with the religious pluralism that is my topic? First of all, this analysis of the shortcomings in both our liturgical life and in the character of personal piety has been validated over and over in conversations with those who found themselves leaving the churches (and a few the synagogues) and joining a community from a quite different religious tradition. I was amused and a bit chagrined to find that none left for theological reasons. It was not the pull of a new interpretation of themselves, their world, or their destiny that lured them! Nor was it a new set of ethical insights or obligations—although issues of life-style and of personal discipline, as shall be seen in a moment, were certainly relevant.

Rather, in each case it was in the general area of spirituality that their interests were first quickened and their loyalty maintained. Specifically, it was by beginning to participate in yoga exercises and meditation (or, correspondingly in Zen groups, by doing Zazen meditation) that they found themselves greatly helped, their lives rather dramatically rearranged, and, above all, that once in, they literally, as one said, could not stay away. When I asked them *what* it was that they found there in these processes of meditative exercise, all agreed that, first, they felt real inside, real as a personal identity (as one person put it, "Because I experience here the unity of myself with my body"); second, they felt part of a genuine and supportive community; and third, because through these meditative practices they experienced a vastly "higher self," or, in other language, the presence in them-

112

selves of the Divine energy. (This is Sikh language and would not be used by the Zen, but the principle of the transcendence of the ordinary self is the same.)

After this positive witness, most of them add that it was *this* that they had missed—although they did not then know that they did—in their former religious communities. The patterns of worship, so they felt, were merely traditional and had little personal or creative meaning. There was, as one said, no experiencing of the divine available, "only faith" and the affirmations of faith. Most important, however, was that they were never urged, told, or advised to *do* anything with regard to their personal life or life-style or taught to develop new habits of personal piety. "There was nothing we could *do* to aid us on the religious path, to move us forward in spiritual development." Or, as another put it, "All I was told was to believe and to do good—but that left me unchanged inside. Here I was shown how to begin, how to move from stage to stage—and the difference for my inner self, and for my experiencing of the divine, has been immense." Such comments came from mainline Protestants, from Catholics, from Jews, and from conservative Evangelicals—with, of course, the appropriate changes in their descriptions of their former religious communities.

If these reports are accurate, then they do validate, provisionally, our analysis of the crisis in common worship and in personal piety in our churches. If in turn this is so, then it has many implications for the role of the pastor as servant in our present situation. For surely it means that if pastors are to be effective servants of their congregations (and of the world), then they must start in the area of spirituality, of the cure and nurture of souls, of the development of personal experiencing of the religious and of God. The servant pastor must not only be preacher, counselor, and ethical adviser (as well as organizer and money-raiser), but also, above all, "spiritual leader," one who can lead his or her community from the beginning of the spiritual life through its many stages to some form of fruition. This has been one of the classic roles of the pastor; it has tended to vanish since the Enlightenment. We now see that it must return in force if the religious strength of the churches is to be maintained.

Positive Suggestions from Other Ways: Pastor as Spiritual Leader

The presence in power of alternative forms in religion can uncover the weaknesses and omissions in ourselves. It can also provide us, if we are open to the assets that they manifestly possess, with positive suggestions for dealing with these omissions. This seems almost disloyal at first: how can a Christian congregation accept suggestions from the forms and practices of another religion? Two things may be said in reply. First, a goodly part of the omissions that these other forms of faith have rediscovered in recent times—in India and Japan, for example—has been by adopting suggestions about emphases in belief, about relevant ethical principles, about forms of worship and of congregational life, and about new and creative relations to the world, from competing Christian congregations. It is not demeaning for us to do the same.

Second, the theological assumptions that lie back of the attitude above—"How can Christians accept suggestions from another religion?"—constitute the exclusivist viewpoint traditional to our faith but at present, as theological affirmations, repudiated by some and certainly by me. If there be truth and grace outside Christianity, if, therefore, these other ways do have something from God to offer *us*, then there is every reason to accept and to use, albeit also to transform, the practices, emphases, and techniques that, apparently, have such healing and renewing power today.

Thus, the most important suggestions in this essay for the pastoral vocation—for the servant ministry today—is that the pastor view himself or herself as a *spiritual leader* and that, as

114

a consequence, he or she present to members of the congregation techniques for the development of their spiritual existence. Many such techniques long used by other traditions are now available; and many of these have, for some time, been practiced by Christians deeply involved with them. Strangely, seminaries and graduate schools, high on theology, ethics, and the techniques of preaching, are generally barren of these aspects of the religious life and religious leadership. The presence of these groups around us is, therefore, genuinely an opportunity to learn from them in areas in which we are lacking and they are rich. Possibly through the development of these new ways of practicing the religious life, we may become strong enough to return to our own traditional ways—unavailable to us now—and adapt them to our present spiritual situation.

One final word on this point. The reintroduction in the theology of the twentieth century of the Reformation emphasis on the priority of grace, on the inadequacy of works, and on the futility of all self-help techniques (one can think of the long diatribes against "all works righteousness" written by nearly every one of the "greats" of the neoorthodox period!) has made many of us wary of techniques for the spirit. How, if we believe in *grace*, can we hope to bring its presence about by doing something, by repeated practices, by techniques? This question represents an interesting theological problem we cannot explore here. Still, there are a couple of things that can be said in reply.

First, a study of the biographies of the Reformation "saints," of the Puritans, and, as I have noted, of typical evangelicals shows that despite the immense emphasis on grace within each of these movements, the lives of these recipients of grace were filled with important religious *practices:* the reading of scripture, personal devotions, a religiously determined life-style, and so on. Outwardly, their lives were not religiously incognito at all. In contrast, there remain few religious practices, except attendance at worship service, that in the same manner feed the inner spirituality of most contemporary clerical persons and laypersons. If the new religious groups show us how vital such practices are, so also does the history of our own traditions.

Second, there can be little question that modern interpretations of grace, however much they may emphasize inner spirituality, find much more place for human response and activity than did the founders of the Reformation. There is hardly a modern theologian who does not make central the responding acknowledgment and decision of faith, the self-direction within the new life, and the responsibility of the new self for itself and its actions. From innumerable modern sources (especially the Enlightenment) a new emphasis on the freedom and the self-constitution, the autonomy of the self, has appeared in theology. This new emphasis on human response, on the personal, has reshaped recent theologies of grace into new forms, forms in which personal decision and action *combine with* grace rather than are ruled by it. Thus, the apparent contradiction of practice, works, and self-help with a theology of grace is in contemporary theology more seeming than real. Responsive action on our part and the nurture of the soul through practice are both warranted if our *existence*, as well as our *thoughts*, is to be suffused with grace and with the experience and consciousness of grace. An emphasis on spirituality and the practices that lead toward it is not antithetical to the workings of grace; it may be that which makes those workings within us more effective.

Theological Implications of Plurality

I want to conclude this essay on plurality and the pastoral vocation with some brief comments on the theological implications of plurality—since the pastor also wonders about theological questions and is dependent, implicitly or ex-

116

plicitly, on answers to those questions. It cannot be over-emphasized how *new* these issues are, and thus how few guidelines from tradition, even from the tradition of early twentieth-century theology, there are. Thus, this is literally an uncharted sea; few have yet ventured out on it, and the early maps of those hardy souls who have are still far from satisfactory. Let us, then, look at some of these problems, at the rocks and the monsters "out there," and see what we can begin to make of them.

As I have noted, one can discern three stages, so to speak, in the church's relation to other religions. (1) There is the stage of clear exclusivism: other ways are simply false, if not blasphemous; Christianity represents, therefore, the only way to salvation. There is neither truth nor grace without it. (2) God works universally, and thus there is some measure of truth and of grace, even a saving measure, in other faiths. The definitive faith, however, the final revelation among all, is in Christ. Thus is it the criterion for all the others, even if it is not the exclusive locus of divine grace, for the love known in Christ is present outside the influence of Christ. This is the view of the liberal tradition and, interestingly, most of the neoorthodox. Both traditions were implicitly, if not explicitly, universalist, and yet both insisted on the finality of Jesus Christ. If one makes the appropriate theological changes, this general position also represents the view of Hinduism and of Buddhism on other faiths; to both of them, other religions are "ways" or "paths" on the journey to truth and Nirvana (or Mohksa). But it is, of course, Hindu or Buddhist enlightenment that defines that journey and its goal. In this sense there is still no *parity* among "ways." At this second stage, therefore, all serious paths or ways are true and in their own way effective; but one among them is taken to be absolute, the defining criterion for the others.

It is my contention that even this second stage is unsatisfactory. It does not represent parity; it sets one faith clearly

117

above the others; and it defines every other viewpoint in the categories of that one. The theological question is, therefore, how does one move to the third stage to affirm the religious pluralism of which the Christian church is one facet, that is, to affirm *parity*. The dilemma, of course, is that every faith proceeds theologically on the basis of some central starting point, some absolute ground or locus of interpretation, some standpoint from which all else is viewed and understood. For Christians, this is the event of Jesus Christ; for Jews, the Torah and the interpretive existence of the community; for Hindus and Buddhists, the "higher consciousness" in relation to the scriptures and traditions of their community; and so on. If one relativizes each of these starting points, how can one proceed to reflect on the world from the point of view of one's religious faith, which is the task of theology? How can one relativize an absolute starting point? Can there be such a combination of relativity and absoluteness, of standing *here* and yet recognizing other places to stand?

Let us note that this question goes deeper than the issue of the relativity of theology and so of doctrines and of dogmas. It has long been recognized that there are no absolute and timeless propositions, even the ones the church officially makes. All are relative to their cultural setting and to their epoch, not to mention to the class, race, and sex from which they emanated. Thus, there is a *history* of theology; and thus, theology must be "brought up to date" and set within the categories relevant to our epoch and place. All this is now recognized. It has relativized every form of theology within the Christian community. It also made possible and fruitful the ecumenical movement. Are we not here dealing with the same problem, only now extended out to other faiths as well as other "denominations"?

The answer is, no; the issue here is far deeper. For in the case of the former "relativizing," it is the human responses to final revelation (in Jesus the Christ) that were relativized, not the revelation itself. Those who freely admitted the historicity of their own theologies, the liberals and the neoorthodox, nevertheless insisted on the absoluteness of Christianity or the finality and *Einmaligkeit* of the event of Jesus Christ. They had no sense of the relativity of that revelation or event of revelation among other revelations. If, however, one grants *parity* to each faith, then this is precisely what one is doing. It is not just our response to revelation that is relative; it is the revelation to which we are responding that is now roughly equal to the others. This is the new situation, a new and deeper interweaving of the relative and the absolute.

As is evident, this new situation represents a genuine puzzle. Let me suggest, however, that difficult as it is to *think* one's way out of it, still there are times when we *act* our way out of it, when what cannot be resolved in theory is nevertheless resolved in practice. For example, in dialogue between diverse religious faiths a new combination of relativity and absoluteness of standing firmly in one's own place and yet seeing its relativity is enacted. I recall vividly many conversations with my Buddhist philosopher friend, Yoshinori Takeuchi, in Kyoto. Once he said to me:

> I do not wish you to cease being a Christian, just as you do not wish me to cease representing Buddhism. This is the condition of our dialogue, that we each continue to stand where we stand. If we cease to be Christian and Buddhist, and each becomes secular, then there will result a different, and much more boring, conversation between us. Yet we each recognize the presence of truth and grace in the other and that recognition of equality is *also* the condition of our dialogue.

Here was a puzzling but fruitful union of a relativizing of one's position on the one hand and yet a firm affirmation of that particular religious viewpoint on the other. If either the firmness of affirmation or the sense of its relativity in relation to the other were to be lost, the dialogue would cease. Per-

119

haps, therefore, we should start here, in our experience of constructive dialogue, and from that puzzling point of unity of what is relative with what is absolute, try to think out a new Christian theology of the encounter of faiths.

The new reality of pluralism, however, does not merely present us with theological problems and puzzles, although it surely does that. As in church life, it also presents us with creative possibilities. For when we begin to explore existence from within another faith, we can see how deeply it can help us wherever we are ourselves weak. Let me give just one example among many.

It has become increasingly evident in the past few decades that the Western view of nature is in sore need of repair. Or, to put this point more specifically, it has been this view of nature that has incited and allowed, even encouraged, the industrial exploitation of nature, which is such a danger to our world and to us. This Western view of nature is not solely the fault of the biblical and the Christian tradition, as some maintain. But, clearly, that tradition is in part responsible. For in its view, humankind is distinguished from and set between God and the natural world. A three-level universe is thus imaged with God above, humans just below, and nature as the mere backdrop or stage on which the drama of the relation between the other two is played out. That this image has been creative, there can be little doubt. It has been the source of the sense of the significance of history; even more, it has been the deepest root of the emphasis on the uniqueness of the human, on the value and power of the human, and so it has been the source of the creative humanitarianism of the modern Western tradition in our social, political, and ethical life.

Nevertheless, this view of nature as *below ourselves*, as subject to our domination, and thus as the mere stage for the really significant action of history, has teamed up with the *objectifying* of nature introduced by the new science. Nature, in this view, is not only distinguished from the human, and so from the realm of grace; it is also transformed into merely a system of objects, a passive, vacuous, and in itself valueless realm to be used by us for our creative purposes. As Dewey said, "We bring purposes and ends to nature; we give her values which she does not in herself have." Such is the theory. The practice has been exploitation.

No one is so optimistic as to think that, on the one hand, a new view of nature will prevent, by itself, the continuing exploitation of nature or that a new view can simply be constructed, so to speak, by fiat. On the other hand, there is little question that different attitudes do make a significant difference, as changing attitudes toward other races and religions show. And there is also little question that the sense of the human relation to nature is very different in other religious traditions than it has been in our own. As an example, the Buddhist feels himself or herself to be a participating part of the whole cycle of nature, since it is taken for granted that during other incarnations each of "us" has been a participant in several parts of nature, of the animal, and even of the plant kingdoms. While the uniqueness of the human level in other religions is perhaps less evident than in the Christian traditions, still there is the clear advantage that the line between the human and the rest of nature is much less sharply drawn. In Buddhism, for example, nature is by no means merely subservient to human purposes; rather, nature has its own integrity and its own destiny, one in which we humans can participate in order to fulfill our own destinies. It is, therefore, a destiny with which we should cooperate. This sense of nature as a wider realm of mutual participation, as a vast cycle of existence through which we all pass, is close to the sense of nature the ecologists give us when they speak of the total natural system on which we are all dependent. And this sense of the wholeness and value of nature is as much a part of the truth as is the uniqueness of the human over against the rest of nature. Our Christian, as well as our cultural, traditions can well learn, therefore, from these religious movements that now make up our new plurality. As with the issue of spirituality, many of these movements have forms of wisdom that Christians sorely need. They present us not only with uncomfortable and taxing challenges, but also with great opportunities for growth.

One final word: the confrontation with plurality in the sharp sense of parity is at present a very real fact in the life of contemporary churches. They would be well advised to face up to this reality and learn from it, rather than to avoid it or struggle against it. As everything I have here stated indicates, however, this problem is not only for the churches and for religious traditions; it will soon be a problem on an even deeper scale for our Western cultural life. For, if what I have said is true, Western culture will soon have to face its *own* context of plurality, the parity of competing cultural forms represented by other areas of the present world. Western scientific and naturalistic culture, which once thought itself to be the one chosen form of future cultural life, now finds itself only one of the many forms of "modern" cultural life functioning in our world; and almost certainly, the strength and lure of new alternative forms will grow in the next decades. Soon we shall not be able to think of "Westernizing" other cultures— for that is not what happens in fact. Thus, in a short period the reality of cultural pluralism will be as evident to Western academia as it is now to the leadership of the religions of the world. It is no small part of the servant task of the churches, therefore, to help prepare their people and our common secular society for this even deeper onslaught of pluralism.[1]

Notes

Introduction

1. Earl E. Shelp and Ronald H. Sunderland, eds., *A Biblical Basis for Ministry* (Philadelphia: Westminster Press, 1981).
2. Earl E. Shelp and Ronald H. Sunderland, eds., *The Pastor as Prophet* (New York: The Pilgrim Press, 1985).
3. Earl E. Shelp and Ronald H. Sunderland, eds., *The Pastor as Priest* (New York: The Pilgrim Press, scheduled for 1987).
4. We do not address here the issue of the preexistence of Christ and the implications of this belief for the subjects of servant ministry or Christology. The question is thoroughly explored in competent works on Christology. Its relevance to servant ministry is considered too remote to warrant digression.
5. The earliest formulation of Jesus as prophet, priest, and king may be from Eusebius of Caesarea. In explaining the relation of Christ to the prophets, priests, and kings of Israel, Eusebius wrote: "Moreover, we are told respecting the prophets, that some were typical Christs, by reason of their unction; so that all these have a reference to the true Christ, the divine and heavenly word, the only high priest of all men, the only king of all creation, and the Father's only supreme Prophet of the prophets." Eusebius Pamphilus, *Ecclesiastical History*, I.3 (Grand Rapids, MI: Baker Book House, 1955). Representative interpretations of the offices of Christ may be found in Charles Hodge, *Systematic Theology*, II (London: Thomas Nelson & Sons, 1873); Albrecht Ritschl, *The Christian Doctrine of Justification and Reconciliation*, ed., H.R. Mackintosh and A.B. Macaulay (Edinburgh: T & T Clark, 1900); and Dale Moody, *The Word of Truth* (Grand Rapids, MI: Wm. B. Eerdmans, 1981).
6. W.A. Visser 't Hooft, *The Kingship of Christ* (New York: Harper & Brothers, 1948).
7. Ibid., p. 100.

Chapter 1. The Servant Dimension of Pastoral Ministry in Biblical Perspective

1. Cf. G.E. Mendenhall, *Law and Covenant in Israel and the Ancient Near East* (Pittsburgh: Presbyterian Board of Colportage, 1955), pp. 33–34.
2. Paul Tillich, *Systematic Theology*, vol. 1 (Chicago: University of Chicago Press, 1951).
3. Confessions I.1.
4. For a more detailed discussion of the theological meaning of the Servant in Second Isaiah, see P.D. Hanson, *The People Called: The Growth of Community in the Bible* (New York: Harper & Row, 1985), ch. 5.
5. Dietrich Bonhoeffer, *The Cost of Discipleship*, tr. R.H. Fuller (London: SCM Press, 1959), p. 86.
6. For a discussion that raises similar issues by applying the image of the "priest" to the medical profession, see David Barnard, "The Physician as Priest, Revisited," forthcoming in *The Journal of Religion and Health*.
7. Ministry carried out on the basis of the model of servanthood does not erode the effectiveness of the minister, or even the authority (understood in the proper sense) of the minister. Authority and leadership are threatened by this model only if they are oriented toward the self-interests of the individual minister, rather than toward God's universal reign of peace and justice. Forms of authority and leadership that are self-serving should be supplanted as readily as possible, functioning most often as they do to disguise incompetence and insecurity. True authority in the servant ministry is a mediated authority. Being the property of no individual, it is open to the scrutiny of all, and thus capable of empowering a community without elevating some members at the cost of others.
8. J.L. Adams, "The Vocation of Ministry," Lowell Lecture, Harvard Divinity School, June 5, 1985.
9. Suggestions for further reading: G. von Rad, *Old Testament Theology*, II (New York: Harper & Row, 1965), pp. 237–62; C. Westermann, *Isaiah 40—66: A Commentary* (Philadelphia: Westminster Press, 1969), pp. 253–69; "servant" and "The Servant of the Lord," *Interpreter's Dictionary of the Bible*, IV

(Nashville: Abingdon Press, 1962), pp. 291–94; C.R. North, *The Suffering Servant in Deutero-Isaiah: An Historical and Critical Study* (London: Oxford University Press, 1948); W. Zimmerli and J. Jeremias, *The Servant of God* (Naperville, IL: A.R. Allenson, 1957); E.F. Sutcliffe, *Providence and Suffering in the Old and New Testaments* (London: Thomas Nelson & Sons, 1953); W. Eichrodt, *Theology of the Old Testament*, II (Philadelphia: Westminster Press, 1967), pp. 231–67; and P.D. Hanson, *The People Called: The Growth of Community in the Bible* (New York: Harper & Row, 1985).

Chapter 2. The Character of Servanthood

1. Theodor Gomperz, *Greek Thinkers*, I (New York: Humanities Press, 1955), p. 72.
2. Ibid., p. 405.
3. Ibid., IV, p. 322.
4. D.B. Davis, *The Problem of Slavery in the Age of Revolution* (Ithaca, NY: Cornell University Press, 1955), p. 40.
5. Gomperz, II, p. 15 (see also I, p. 404).
6. Gomperz, IV, pp. 324–25.
7. Davis, pp. 39, 42.
8. G.W.F. Hegel, *The Phenomenology of Mind* (London: George Allen & Unwin, 1964), pp. 234, 236–37.
9. Jürgen Moltmann, *The Crucified God* (New York: Harper & Row, 1974), p. 27.
10. W. Zimmerli, in W. Zimmerli and J. Jeremias, *The Servant of God* (London: SCM Press, 1957), pp. 13–14; see also George A.F. Knight, *A Christian Theology of the Old Testament* (London: SCM Press, 1959), p. 189.
11. Zimmerli, p. 14.
12. If the term slave appears to be too stark a referent in this context, it probably had the same impact on the disciples when used by Jesus—despite their familiarity with the image in Isaiah and elsewhere!
13. D.M. Smith, "Theology and Ministry in John," in *A Biblical Basis for Ministry*, ed. E.E. Shelp and R.H. Sunderland (Philadelphia: Westminster Press, 1981), p. 217.

14. Moltmann, p. 9.
15. Gustav Stahlin, "Skandalon, skandalizō," in *Theological Dictionary of the New Testament*, VII, ed. G. Kittel and G. Friedrich (Grand Rapids, MI: Wm. B. Eerdmans, 1971), p. 349.
16. Moltmann, pp. 42ff.
17. Ibid., p. 40.
18. General Committee, World Student Christian Federation, "The Christian Community in the Academic World," *Student World*, No. 3, 1965, p. 234.
19. J.L. Segundo, *The Community Called Church* (Maryknoll, New York: Orbis Books, 1973), p. 106.
20. Leslie Newbigin, "Four Talks on I Peter," in *We Were Brought Together*, ed. David Taylor (Sydney, Australia: Australian Council of Churches, 1960), p. 101.
21. Stanley Hauerwas, "The Pastor as Prophet: Ethical Reflections on an Improbable Mission," in *The Pastor as Prophet*, ed. E.E. Shelp and R.H. Sunderland (New York: The Pilgrim Press, 1985), pp. 42–43. Moltmann puts this thought in even stronger terms: faith in a crucified God is capable of setting people free from their cultural illusions, releasing them from the involvements that enslave them, and confronting them with the truth of their own existence and their society. "Before there can be correspondence and agreement between faith and the surrounding world, there must first be the painful demonstration of truth in the midst of untruth. In this pain, we experience reality outside ourselves, which we have not made up or thought out for ourselves. The pain arouses a love which can no longer be indifferent, but seeks out its opposite, which is ugly and unworthy of love, in order to love it." Moltmann, p. 39.
22. See J. Jeremias, *The Parables of Jesus* (London: SCM Press, 1954), pp. 143–44; and T.W. Manson, *The Sayings of Jesus* (London: SCM Press, 1954), p. 249.
23. Schubert Ogden, personal communication, Institute of Religion, March 14, 1985.
24. Ibid.
25. R.H. Sunderland and E.E. Shelp, "Prophetic Ministry: An Introduction," in *The Pastor as Prophet*, ed. E.E. Shelp and R.H. Sunderland (New York: The Pilgrim Press, 1985).

Chapter 3. Justice and the Servant Task of Pastoral Ministry

1. See especially *The Ritual Process* (Hawthorne, New York: Aldine Publishing Co., 1969; El Toro, CA: Pelican Books, 1974). Turner has elaborated the concepts in many subsequent writings.
2. Arnold van Gennep, *The Rites of Passage* (1901; reprint Chicago: University of Chicago Press, 1960).
3. The phrase is suggested by Parker Palmer, *The Company of Strangers* (New York: Crossroad, 1981).
4. Suggestions for additional reading: Tom F. Driver, *Christ in a Changing World: Toward an Ethical Christology* (New York: Crossroad, 1981); Dorothy M. Emmet, *The Moral Prism* (London: Macmillan, 1979); Gerard Fourez, *Liberation Ethics* (Philadelphia: Temple University Press, 1981); James Gustafson, *Protestant and Roman Catholic Ethics* (Chicago: University of Chicago Press, 1978); Beverly W. Harrison, *Our Right to Choose: Toward a New Ethics of Abortion* (Boston: Beacon Press, 1983); Joe Holland and Peter Henriot, *Social Analysis: Linking Faith and Justice* (Maryknoll, NY: Orbis Books, 1983); John MacMurray, *Persons in Relation* (Atlantic Highlands, NJ: Humanities Press, 1961); Brian Mahan and L. Dale Richesin, *The Challenge of Liberation Theology: A First-World Response* (Maryknoll, NY: Orbis Books, 1981); James B. Nelson, *Embodiment: An Approach to Sexuality and Christian Theology* (Minneapolis: Augsburg Publishing House, and New York: The Pilgrim Press, 1978; Palmer Parker, *The Company of Strangers: Christians and the Renewal of America's Public Life* (New York: Crossroad, 1981); Larry L. Rasmussen and Bruce C. Birch, *The Bible and Ethics in the Christian Life* (Minneapolis: Augsburg Publishing House, 1976); Joan L. Segundo, *The Liberation of Theology* (Maryknoll, NY: Orbis Books, 1976); Joan L. Segundo, *The Sacraments Today* (Maryknoll, NY: Orbis Books, 1974); Victor Turner, *From Ritual to Theatre: The Human Seriousness of Play* (New York: Performing Arts Journal Publications, 1982); Victor Turner, "Images of Anti-temporality: An Essay in the Anthropology of Experience," *Harvard Theological Review* 75 (April 1982), pp. 243–65.

Chapter 4. The Servant Church

1. See Ernst Troeltsch, *The Social Teaching of the Christian Churches*, tr. Olive Wyon (New York: Harper Torch Books, 1960); H. Richard Niebuhr, *The Social Sources of Denominationalism* (Cleveland, OH: Meridian Books, 1957); and Peter Paris, *The Social Teaching of the Black Churches* (Philadelphia: Fortress Press, 1985).

2. Williston Walker, *A History of the Christian Church*, rev. ed. (New York: Charles Scribner's Sons, 1959); Carter G. Woodson, *History of the Negro Church* (Washington, DC: Associated Publishers, 1921); E. Franklin Frazier, *The Negro Church in America* (New York: Schocken Books, 1964); and Sydney E. Alstrom, *A Religious History of the American People* (New Haven, CT: Yale University Press, 1972).

3. Karl Barth, *Church Dogmatics*, vol. 4, pt. 1, tr. G.W. Bromiley and T.F. Torrance (Edinburgh: T & T Clark, 1956); ibid., vol. 4, pt. 2; Cyril Richardson, *The Church Through the Centuries* (New York: Charles Scribner's Sons, 1950); Jürgen Moltmann, *The Church in the Power of the Spirit* (New York: Harper & Row, 1977); and Hans Küng, *The Church* (New York: Sheed & Ward, 1967).

4. John Calvin, *Institutes of the Christian Religion*, vol. 2, Library of Christian Classics, tr. F.L. Battles (Philadelphia: Westminster Press, 1960), p. 1023.

5. *The Complete Writings of Menno Simons*, tr. Leonard Verduin (Scottdale, PA: Herald Press, 1956), p. 741.

6. Ibid., p. 746.

7. Calvin, *Institutes*, vol. 2, p. 1025.

8. *Complete Writings of Menno Simons*, p. 752.

9. Franklin H. Littell, *The Origins of Sectarian Protestanism* (New York: Macmillan, 1964), p. 53.

10. See Peter Berger, *The Sacred Canopy* (New York: Doubleday, Anchor Books, 1969).

11. Langdon Gilkey, *How the Church Can Minister to the World Without Losing Itself* (New York: Harper & Row, 1964), p. 71.

12. James Gustafson, *The Church as Moral Decision-Maker* (New York: The Pilgrim Press, 1970), p. 63.

13. Ibid., pp. 122–23.

14. Ibid., p. 151.

15. Cited in Olli Alho, *The Religion of the Slaves: A Study of the Religious Tradition and Behavior of Plantation Slaves in the United States, 1830–1865* (Helsinki: Soumalainen Tiedeakatemia, 1976), p. 140.
16. Ibid., p. 170.
17. Ibid., p. 125.
18. Although liberation theology is largely associated with the continent of Latin America, it is important to emphasize that similar developments are found in the churches and theologies of Africa and Asia and among minorities and women in the United States. The best sources for an examination of these theologies and their relationship to one another are the books that have been produced by the Ecumenical Association of Third World Theologians (EATWOT). EATWOT was organized in 1976 in Tanzania and has held subsequent meetings in other countries of the Third World, focusing on African, Asian, and Latin-American liberation theologies. See Sergio Torres and Virginia Fabella, eds., *The Emergent Gospel* (Maryknoll, NY: Orbis Books, 1978); Kofi Appiah-Kubi and Sergio Torres, eds., *African Theology En Route* (Maryknoll, NY: Orbis Books, 1979); Virginia Fabella, ed., *Asia's Struggle for Full Humanity* (Maryknoll, NY: Orbis Books, 1980); Sergio Torres and John Eagleson, eds., *The Challenge of Basic Christian Communities* (Maryknoll, NY: Orbis Books, 1981); and Virginia Fabella and Sergio Torres, eds., *Irruption of the Third World* (Maryknoll, NY: Orbis Books, 1983). Orbis Books is well known for its publication of books on liberation theologies in the Third World and also among minorities in the United States.
19. See Leonardo Boff, *Jesus Christ Liberator*, tr. Patrick Hughes (Maryknoll, NY: Orbis Books, 1978); Hugo Echegaray, *The Practice of Jesus*, tr. M.J. O'Connell (Maryknoll, NY: Orbis Books, 1980); James H. Cone, *God of the Oppressed* (New York: Seabury Press, 1975); Bishop Joseph A. Johnson Jr., "Jesus Christ: Liberator," in his *The Soul of the Black Preacher* (New York: The Pilgrim Press, 1971).
20. See Jürgen Moltmann, *The Crucified God* (New York: Harper & Row, 1974).
21. Paulo Freire, *Pedagogy of the Oppressed* (New York: Herder & Herder, 1970), p. 35.

22. Arthur Simon, *Bread for the World*, rev. ed. (New York: Paulist Press; Grand Rapids, MI: Wm. B. Eerdmans, 1984), p. 7.
23. Ibid., p. 144.
24. Hugo Assmann, *Theology for a Nomad Church*, tr. Paul Burns (Maryknoll, NY: Orbis Books, 1975), p. 81.
25. Max Weber, *The Sociology of Religion*, tr. Ephraim Fischoff (Boston: Beacon Press, 1964), p. 106.
26. Ibid., p. 107.
27. Ibid.
28. Ibid., p. 108.

Chapter 5. The Service of Theology to the Servant Task of Pastoral Ministry

1. Victor Paul Furnish, *II Corinthians* (Garden City, NY: Doubleday, 1984), p. 306. See also by the same author, "The Ministry of Reconciliation," *Currents in Theology and Mission* 4 (1977), 204–18; and "Theology and Ministry in the Pauline Letters," in *A Biblical Basis for Ministry*, ed. E.E. Shelp and Ronald H. Sunderland (Philadelphia: Westminster Press, 1981), pp. 101–44, 234–36.
2. See Gerhard Ebeling, *Wort Gottes und Tradition, Studien zu einer Hermeneutik der Konfessionen* (Göttingen: Vandenhoeck & Ruprecht, 1964), pp. 115–17; also Albert C. Outler, *The Christian Tradition and the Unity We Seek* (New York: Oxford University Press, 1957), pp. 105–42.
3. See Vincent Brümmer, *Theology and Philosophical Inquiry: An Introduction* (Philadelphia: Westminster Press, 1982), pp. 9–33.
4. See Jürgen Habermas, "Was heisst Universalpragmatik?" in *Sprachpragmatik und Philosophie*, ed. K.-O. Apel (Frankfurt: Suhrkamp Verlag, 1976), pp. 224–25.
5. See Nicholas Wolterstorff, "On God Speaking," *The Reformed Journal*, July–August 1969, p. 11.
6. Schubert M. Ogden, *The Point of Christology* (San Francisco: Harper & Row, 1982), pp. 20–40.
7. See Habermas, "Was heisst Universalpragmatik?" pp. 249–55.
8. See ibid., p. 253.

Chapter 6. Plurality: Our New Situation

1. The following are suggested readings on religious plurality: John B. Cobb Jr., *Beyond Dialogue* (Philadelphia: Fortress Press, 1982); Charles Davis, *The Christian and Other Religions* (New York: Herder & Herder, 1971); John Hick and B. Hebblethwaite, eds., *Christianity and Other Religions* (Philadelphia: Fortress Press, 1980); John Hick, *God and the Universe of Faiths* (New York: St. Martin's Press, 1973); John Hick, ed., *Truth and Dialogue in World Religions* (Philadelphia: Westminster Press, 1974); John Hick, *God Has Many Names* (London: Macmillan, 1980); Paul Knitter, *No Other Name?* (Maryknoll, NY: Orbis Books, 1985); R. Panikkar, *The Unknown Christ of Hinduism* (New York: Paulist Press, 1979); R. Panikkar, *Myth, Faith, and Hermeneutics* (New York: Paulist Press, 1979); W.C. Smith, *The Meaning and End of Religion* (New York: New American Library, 1964); W.C. Smith, *Towards a World Theology* (Philadelphia: Westminster Press, 1981); and F. Schuon, *The Transcendent Unity of Religions* (New York: Harper & Row, 1975).

131